My Mother, the Bunny, and Me

A Memoir by Edith Kunhardt Davis

Acknowledgments

Through the decades, various members of the Kunhardt family also have felt compelled to write about my mother's life and her famous children's book, *Pat the Bunny*. She herself started off with the unfinished and never-published "The Family Book." Others have continued by publishing books and articles, and producing a TV documentary. Some of my material is drawn from those sources.

To my beloved daughter, Martha Knapp Davis,

who was my main reader and copyeditor

Family Photo

Cowboy Costume

Chapter One: The Thirties

In Which I Was Born

My mother, Dorothy Kunhardt, wrote the children's book *Pat the Bunny* at the end of the Great Depression. She had been writing children's books to earn money for our family since my father lost his job as a textile executive after the Crash of 1929. I was the baby of the family for whom she wrote the book, as well as its first "reader." *Pat the Bunny* is based on her observations of me as a baby and toddler, and it has been a part of my life for as long as I can remember.

When I was born in 1937, between the Stock Market Crash and the Second World War, our family lived in a simple wooden Victorian house on the side of a steep, wild hill in New Jersey. The family consisted of Dorothy, my father, Philip, and Nancy, Phil Jr., and Ken, who were 11, 10, and 7. We had a dog, Hundred, who was named for his number of spots, and called Hundie for short.

The family lore was that my brother Ken got me by holding his breath while passing a graveyard, which was a potent way of making a wish. For years my siblings had been wishing for a baby. They wished when they blew out their birthday cake candles, they wished on every hay wagon, and of course they wished on every wishbone of every chicken or turkey or duck they ate. Finally this wish came true.

When I was a week old, Dad brought my siblings to the hospital to see me. Often the mother and baby were hospitalized for weeks after the birth.

My brother, Phil Jr., had written a poem to celebrate the occasion:

> I needith
> My edith
> Or I'll bleedith.
> I'll give her milk
> And wrap her
> In blankets and silk.

The nurse rolled a little crib up close to the glass door, and in it was a tiny baby. I was lying on my stomach with my face turned almost straight into the mattress.

"Can the nurse hold her up?" asked Phil Jr. "I can't see her face one bit." But the nurse didn't want to wake me, because then I would just cry for two hours because my suppertime was two hours away and the rule was no picking up babies at the wrong time.

After three weeks in the hospital, a normal amount of time in those days, I was brought home in the car. My siblings were lined up in the driveway to greet me. "Now she's really ours," Nancy said as I was carried into the house.

My mother carefully recorded my measurements in "The Annals of Babyhood," an ornate leather-bound baby record book that I still own. It seems that I was premature. My mother was 42 years old when I was born; perhaps that was why I was born early and was small. These days, 5 pounds 14 ounces wouldn't be considered premature, but 42 years old is still considered late to have a baby, and, indeed, she had a miscarriage the next year.

> *Annals of Babyhood*
> Name: Edith Turner Kunhardt
> Born: September 30, 1937
> Weight: 5:14

Weight: went down to 5:9
Regained birth weight October 12
1st formula: 5 oz. Borden's
Evaporated Milk
13 oz. water

When I was about two months old, my mother received a letter from the Park Avenue doctor who had delivered me:

"Dear Mrs. Kunhardt:

"Baby's blood was only 68% and while that is not at all alarming it does, none the less, denote a mild anemia which is not at all uncommon in premature babies at the tenth or twelfth week. Accordingly would you be good enough to start the iron, for which a prescription is enclosed. Work up gradually to the twenty drops, which should be given in orange juice with the cod liver oil concentrate."

Waiting for me at the house on the hill besides my family was my nanny. A few weeks before, Dad had gone to the employment agency muttering that he was going to hire a strapping young Scandinavian nurse with lots of experience who would work from morning to night; the boys and Nancy had been such a handful. Several previous nannies had been bad-tempered and gruff, and they had to go, but there was one named Anna whom my siblings loved. When Anna had to leave because the three children were too old to have her anymore, Nancy made Anna breathe into a bottle and kept the bottle on her bureau for years.

Dad returned from the agency with a new nanny named Lilly. She was utterly beguiling, and he couldn't resist hiring her. She was sixty-five years old, four feet ten inches tall, with a gray permanent wave. She came from Birmingham, England, and had been married to a sea captain who had died. She had a daughter and a son who lived in New Jersey, and she had never been a nanny before. When I began to talk, I couldn't pronounce "Lilly" but gargled out "Yoyo" instead. Soon everyone, even strangers, called her "Yoyo."

Years of strictness had been imposed on my older siblings by my mother and enforced by past nannies. They had rigid bedtimes and were forced to sit at the table until they ate everything on their plates. They were made to wear metal thumb covers so they wouldn't suck their thumbs, and their hands were tied to their cribs for the same reason. This was what the culture required at the time. With me, however, my mother was ready to let loose. When I cried, she picked me up any old time, something forbidden with the other children, and she let me sit on Dad's lap at the breakfast table and eat honey that came from his own beehive from his finger.

My mother wrote about my first mornings at home:

"Every morning Dad went over to the bassinet where the baby was lying saying, 'Ah, Ah,' and spanking her lips together, and he would always give her his rolled-up socks that he had just got from his bureau drawer. He always let her hold them for a minute. At first it was a second instead of a minute because her hands just opened and shut and opened and shut as if the electricity was being turned off and on, off and on and she didn't know how to grab anything and keep it. But Dad said he enjoyed his day better if she just held his socks for him even for a second in the morning."

Then he would pick me up from my bassinet and carry me downstairs to sit on his knee at breakfast. Well, really, tucked under his arm. He tucked me next to his body with my right arm stretched around onto his back. Mum had to butter his toast for him because he couldn't use two hands, and every time he bent over for a bite of egg and bacon I bent over with him until my face almost went into the plate.

As the weeks went on I grew so fat and large that Dad could not tuck me under his arm at breakfast anymore. I sat on his knee and held myself up with my own back. I was always smiling. Everybody said they had never seen such a happy baby. Mum noted, "That's because she's a baby that is just loved till she's almost torn in little pieces. It's good for a baby to be loved like that."

It was true. My brothers were always trying to pull and even yank me away from my sister Nancy's lap, and then one of them would pull my legs and the other one would pull my arms, trying to get me all for himself. They quarreled over me and shouted, "Let go! You know it's my turn!"

I smiled straight through everything. Mum wrote, "I've brought up three babies by rule and now I'm going to have fun and so is everybody else."

After breakfast, Dad often carried me into the living room and, with Mum, Nancy, Phil Jr., and Ken joining him in singing a waltzing tune, he whirled me up over his head and swooped me down near waist height. Then he held me in a dancing position, cupping one of my tiny hands in his and cradling me against his big Harvard Varsity Football Team chest. When I was a tiny baby I just hung in his hands quietly, like a doll. When I got a little older, about six months, I began to kick my feet in the air and dance, too, and giggle with joy. The other children and Mum always joined the singing, and even if they had not finished breakfast before the dance, they jumped up from their seats and ran into the living room when they heard Dad sing out the first note. At first Mum tried to admonish them from her place at the head of the dining room table, begging, "Sit down, children. Don't leave the table till you've finished eating," but she said it so faintly and lamely that everyone knew she didn't mean it, especially as she was halfway into the living room herself and already singing.

By the time *Pat the Bunny* was published in the fall of 1940, my mother had observed me for two and a half years. She carried a pad with her all the time, or she wrote on scraps of paper napkins, old envelopes, anything she could find as she labored on descriptions of my development, anecdotes of my discoveries, and lists of things that I did. Mostly she worked late at night, when everyone else was asleep. Her little workroom was under the naked wooden beams of the roof in our attic. The workroom was unheated, and dangerous portable heaters glowed there in the winter. In the summer it was so stifling that she tied handkerchiefs around her wrists to keep the sweat from running down her arms and smudging her work. Of course, air conditioning did not exist at the time. It was in her workroom that she got the idea for a new children's book that she would write and illustrate.

The title would be an action verb. "Pat," it urged, "the bunny."

The text would be very simple. Here it is in its entirety: "Here are Paul and Judy. They can do lots of things. You can do lots of things, too.

"Judy can pat the bunny. Now YOU pat the bunny.

"Judy can play peek-a-boo with Paul. Now YOU play peek-a-boo with Paul.

"Paul can smell the flowers. Now YOU smell the flowers.

"Judy can look in the mirror. Now YOU look in the mirror.

"Judy can feel Daddy's scratchy face. Now YOU feel Daddy's scratchy face.

"Paul can put his finger through Mummy's ring. Now YOU put your finger through Mummy's ring.

"That's all. Bye-bye. Can you say Bye-bye? Paul and Judy are waving Bye-bye to YOU."

These simple repeated words, addressed directly to the child, and the physical actions the child is encouraged to make marked a new way that small children would interact with literature. Full of deep knowledge of a child's earliest developmental states, *Pat the Bunny* was clearly an innovation, not least for appealing to the senses. Patting the bunny and touching Daddy's scratchy face address one sense, touch. Playing peek-a-boo, looking in the mirror, and "reading" Judy's Book address another sense, sight. Smelling the flowers engages the sense of smell. The first edition included a doll with a squeaker, which drew on a fourth sense, hearing, but the squeaker was removed because it was made of rubber from Japan. After the Japanese attacked Pearl Harbor in 1941 and the U.S. entered World War II, the entire page was scrapped. In the original book, the only missing sense was taste. My mother ruminated about edible pages, but she never got farther than thinking up a name for her product and mocking up a cover which read, "The Cracker Animal Book: Read Your Book and EAT IT TOO!"

My mother used extra material on most of the pages, an approach that had never been seen before in a book. Alongside using the senses, she invented activities to challenge a young child. He or she, aided by the words, learns that the soft white rabbit-shaped material is for patting. The piece of cloth hiding Paul's face is for lifting up and peeking under. The perfume-impregnated flowers are for smelling, the mirror is for looking at one's reflection, and the ring-shaped hole is for poking one's finger through. The smaller Judy's Book, glued inside the bigger one, is for pretending: to read, to listen to the ticking of a clock, to eat, and to measure oneself by throwing up one's arms and gurgling out, "Soooo Big!"

In order to demonstrate to publishers what she had in mind, my mother fashioned a dummy that was almost identical to the book we know today. She printed each letter and drew every illustration by hand. These sample pages were sewn together with string.

Simon & Schuster agreed to publish the book but wrestled with how to finance the unusual project, a book with moving parts. One way they found to cut costs was to publish it in only two colors. At last the problems were solved and the book was released.

After its appearance in bookstores, the publisher wrote, "*Pat the Bunny* is fast developing into a runaway. It will be impossible to get more than 102,000 copies by Christmas." To meet the huge demand, the binder rented an extra floor in the factory and hired a large force of women who did nothing all day but assemble the book by hand. Later, workers in several printing plants around the U.S. labored simultaneously on the job. Today it is still assembled by hand in China.

Pat the Bunny is known as "the first tactile book," but this doesn't seem to be strictly true. A book called *Cottontails* featured tufts of cotton simulating the tails of illustrated rabbits on its cover. It was brought out by a small publishing house named Scott in 1938, two years before my mother's book appeared, and it went out of print soon after. I don't know if my mother ever saw *Cottontails*. I do know that her inspiration for the bunny was the shape of the crocheted rabbit that my sister Nancy received when the family visited England in 1928.

My brother Ken said that the reason our mother was a good children's book writer was that she had a "baby mind," which was true and a high compliment. She understood children extraordinarily well. When I wrote companion books to *Pat the Bunny* many years later, I realized that my mother had observed the earliest discoveries children make and used them as the foundation of the book. The text and the added materials encourage the child's participation in the actions on each page. They stimulate a wide range of senses. They foster a close relationship with the adult reading it. The child wants to be read to again and again, and the book's use of repetition, along with its gentle cadences, eventually lead to memorizing the words and then to reading it out loud. This is the secret of the book's remarkable longevity—this, and its loving portrayal of a family. The characters Paul and Judy, a brother and sister (named after my second cousins), stand in for the toddler, although some children treasure the book until they are much older. No matter how many times *Pat the Bunny* has been copied (it was the first of the touch-and-feel children's books that later became an industry) or "companioned" as I did, no one has been able to match its brilliance. The book is still a favorite gift for babies and is often given before the baby is born. The words on the back of the original printings described it well: "Dorothy Kunhardt has made this book for the littlest children— those who can't even read yet. It is a small book, easy to handle, with a charming surprise on every page."

Some librarians disliked the book because it seemed to them more like a toy than a book, and because its moving parts made it vulnerable to having children rip them out. Maybe it wasn't a serious book to many librarians at the time, but it was serious to all the children who fell in love with it. By Christmas of 1940, two months after *Pat the Bunny* was published, more than 100,000 copies had been sold and the book was the best-selling juvenile title of the year. It has remained in print for more than 75 years, having sold millions of copies.

Our House

Pat the Bunny's cover is peach and turquoise—distinctive colors as recognizable as the Bunny itself. My mother decorated the cover and inner pages with little freehand dots that became as distinguishing as the strange-looking, somewhat demented flowers on the inner pages.

Chapter Two: The Forties, Part 1

The Hill, the House, and My Family

Our Hill, besides being a hill, was a private estate of more than a thousand acres owned by a wealthy family. Several other families besides mine lived in small rental houses scattered around the property.

On a clear day, you could see the Empire State Building from the Hill. It looked like a stubby thumb sticking up, and was the only thing visible on the horizon. The Hill was 26 miles away from Manhattan as the crow flies, and was part of the Kittatinny Mountain range in New Jersey. Kemble Mountain, the highest peak near our house, was only 545 feet above sea level, but it was precipitous enough to keep the area from being developed. Seventy-five years later, most of the land is still wooded. One of our trees, a Norway spruce, was chosen before I was born to be one of the very first Rockefeller Center Christmas trees.

The Hill was bounded to the south by Mount Kemble Avenue, named for the original landholder, Peter Kemble, who had kept slaves. Western Avenue lay to the north, the Jockey Hollow portion of the Morristown National Historic Park to the west, and Bailey Hollow Road to the east. The estate was about three miles from Morristown, a city of 19,000 people at that time. Originally the estate was larger, consisting of farms and houses on both sides of Mount Kemble Avenue.

Bill and Bertha Jenks, the kindly and generous couple who owned the estate, had suffered reversals during the stock market Crash of 1929. He had been the president of the Cotton Market and had held a seat on the New York Stock Exchange. During the Depression, Bill had to offer for sale their enormous mansion on Mount Kemble Avenue. They moved to a smaller, shingled home at the top of the Hill which had recently been rebuilt after a fire, and which everyone called the Big House. Bill and Bertha were Quakers and spoke in the Plain Language, addressing each other as "Thee" and "Thou."

In its heyday before the Crash and the War, the estate had consisted of four working farms to provide beef, milk, ham, chickens, eggs, and fresh vegetables produced in greenhouses. There was a riding stable, a hay barn, an ice house where blocks of ice were stored year round with sawdust packed around them to slow their melting. In winter, workers cut the blocks from frozen ponds in the region and distributed them to the tenants on the Hill. Smaller chunks went into the icebox that each family had in their kitchen to keep food from spoiling.

Also on the Hill were formal gardens, a tennis court, a rustic goldfish pond with a bridge, and a vista that looked out toward Morristown. There was a spring-fed concrete swimming pool that was more like a pond with an irregular shape, a continuous flow of cold spring water in and out, and moss growing around its perimeter. Bill Jenks had built a series of hydraulic ram pumps that lifted fresh water from the springs into several cisterns, so there was a liberal water supply to the pool and to our houses. The pumps used downhill water pressure to raise water much higher than it was in the springs, and no other power was needed. All these systems, areas, and buildings were still there when my family lived there, but the estate had become run down and crumbling, with only an estate manager/gardener, much beloved by the owners and their family, to take care of the place as best he could.

My father loved his hillside flower garden that he had hacked from the tangle of undergrowth below our house. The flower beds were shaped like scallop shells, like those in the gardens around the mansion in Massachusetts where he had grown up. There were roses, solomon seal, marigolds. Sometimes, when I was playing with him in the garden, he held a buttercup under my chin and asked, "Do you like butter?" Then, peering at the yellow reflection on my skin, he exclaimed ecstatically, "You LOVE butter!" In hot weather, he sat by his flowers wearing only a pair of khaki shorts, his broad back tanned a rich brown, a red kerchief tucked in his belt, and raked the earth with a claw implement. A glass milk bottle full of water leaned against a tree in the shade. Having only one kidney because of a football accident, Dad needed to drink a lot of water.

"Come out, come out," he called to my mother.

"Come in, come in," urged my mother from her perch at the second-story window above.

Neither one stirred. My mother often told us she longed to live in the basement of Rockefeller Center, where she could avoid rain and snow and sleet, and the deer that nightly came out of the woods on our Hill, the raccoons that raided our garbage pail each night, the bats that swooped, and the squirrels that lived and sometimes died and stank in the walls of our small wooden house.

Dad loved nature and sports. He loved climbing mountains, fishing for trout, playing tennis, beekeeping, gardening, and chopping wood, while my mother loved research and ancient dusty books, and inventing new ideas. He had been an athlete in school and used to ski cross-country through the snowy woods between North Andover, Massachusetts, where he grew up, and Groton, his boarding school, which was 35 miles away from his house.

My mother was born in Harlem, Manhattan, so she was a city girl. Her father managed a hotel there. It was the turn of the century, and Harlem was fashionable at the time. Her earliest memory was of sitting on the stoop of their brownstone house and scraping her roller skate key against the steps. Later, she went to Brearley School, a girl's institution in the city, and to Bryn Mawr College in Pennsylvania. She played water polo and field hockey at college, became president of the Christian Association, and after graduation she traveled around the world with her best friend. They reached Egypt just after Tutankhamun's tomb had been discovered and treasures were still being carried out.

Sometimes, when we had the money, we had a live-in cook. Her name was Sophronia, and she was black. Sophie's father had been a slave. She had grown up in Virginia and had 16 brothers and sisters.

Sophie lived in a room in the attic. Once a month she took the train into Manhattan to rest for a weekend and to visit her family. My mother glared as she watched Sophie struggle with a heavy suitcase, much heavier, my mother said, than when she had returned from the city the month before. "She steals our sugar," Mum muttered. "Who knows what else of ours is in there?" she continued, but she never confronted Sophie to her face. I was a little scared of Sophie because she enjoyed sucking on her teeth, which

I thought were false, and I was afraid they'd pop out.

On April Fools Day every year my family gathered at the table and Sophie served us breakfast: popovers with, surprise! wads of cotton inside instead of warm puff pastry, a big recurring joke which we all enjoyed with squeals of laughter every time.

More than twenty year later, at the end of my last phone conversation with her, she confided that she was "the darker one," compared to her brothers and sisters, something which had bothered her since childhood. I was touched that she told me that.

Years later I met her granddaughter, Bucky. She was a bank vice president. We both remembered Sophie's kindness and sense of humor.

Every day at our house started when my father carried a bucket of coal up the cellar steps, grabbed an iron spike, pushed it into a hole in our two-burner coal stove, and rattled it around in the hole. That made a lot of gray and glowing ashes fall down inside. He opened a door in the stove and shoveled the hot ashes out into a pail. Then he removed the caps from the burners and poured shiny, black new lumps of coal into the openings. The stove had a top oven—very hot—

for roasting and a cooler bottom oven for warming plates. A twist of the spigot that stuck out of the front of the stove released boiling water, so you didn't have to heat water for tea or coffee. The stove was on day and night if it was tended carefully. It was manufactured by a company named Aga, and it seemed very special to us.

We spent a lot of time in the kitchen, near the stove and the sink and the icebox. (Years later when there were grandchildren, we had two refrigerators to accommodate all the hungry mouths.) My mother did most of the cooking at that time, and Sophie only came on special occasions. Mum was very good on standing rib roasts, turkeys, and legs of lamb. We all loved baked potatoes and roast potatoes and mashed potatoes with lots of butter. One of the most fun things was to excavate a depression into the top of my pile of mashed potatoes, into which I dipped other foodstuffs. We also ate a lot of "top round ground," which is what we called meatballs. We never had pasta or rice.

My parents didn't have wine with meals, just cocktails like Old Fashioneds, with sweet fruits, before dinner. On Sunday nights we often had turkey a la king made from leftovers, which we teasingly called turkey a la queen. Mum didn't bake, preferring to buy pies and cakes for the special occasions, such as when her parents came out from New York for the day. On Sunday nights my father took over the cooking and we had leftovers, a big salad, and sometimes corned beef hash with a fried egg on top.

My mother's favorite foods were baked cow tongue, soft shell crab, shad roe, and corn on the cob. I thought they were all disgusting, except for the corn. Mum insured the corn's freshness by driving down the Hill to the farm on the other side of Route 202, having phoned first to make sure the corn had just been wrenched from the stalk. Dad's favorite foods were steak and trout that he caught at his fishing club. My favorite treats were raw carrots with salt, oatmeal with salt, meat with jelly, and hot fudge sundaes. My favorite almost-daily food was tomato and lettuce sandwiches on Wonder Bread with lots of Hellman's mayonnaise.

Next to the kitchen there was a small pantry with space for Dad's indoor plants and the liquor bar. In the back of the kitchen, there was another pantry where there was a mangle for squeezing water out of laundry before it was hung outside to dry.

We used the dining room when all of us, parents and children, were home, which was not often. On the wall in a position of honor was a dark Millet-esque oil painting of sheep bathed in reddish evening light in an ornate gold frame. Dad loved the painting but later gave it to Uncle Jack, because he felt obligated to give this family heirloom to his older brother.

Next to the dining room was the front hall and a cupboard where Dad kept his smelly old pipes, his fuzzy pipe cleaners, and pungent tins of tobacco. Next to that was the living room, furnished with dark carpeting, mahogany settees and a sofa with black horsehair coverings. There was a small, more comfortable sofa with a chintz covering and a big armchair with matching cover. Near the door on a table was the telephone, a model with a horn-shaped earpiece hanging from the hook that disconnected the call at the end of the conversation. Our telephone number in its entirety was 2026W. Painted portraits of uncomfortable-looking ancestors hung on the walls. There was a fireplace with a marble mantle, upon which stood beautiful cockatoo parrots made of precious china and lamps with cut-glass dangles. My father's desk, where he paid bills and listened to classical music, was at the back of the living room. (My mother called classical music "noise.") Also there were shelves full from floor to ceiling with books, which my mother collected. She had first editions of J.D. Salinger's *Catcher in the Rye*, Robert Frost's *Collected Poems, The Thurber Carnival* by James Thurber, and Truman Capote's *Other Voices, Other Rooms*. She had met Frost and Capote at a writer's conference. My father's favorite books were by Dickens, William O. Douglas, and one called *Tight Line* about fly fishing.

My brothers Phil and Ken roomed together upstairs in the back bedroom. They were the mischief-makers, and they teased Nancy mercilessly. They realized with glee that she had a fear of death and couldn't bear that all people would go away and never come back again. They dug a full-sized grave, her grave, below the second-floor bathroom window. It was a constant reminder, as the best view was from the toilet seat.

Nancy was furious and terrified by the prank. "Disgusting brothers!" she cried. "I hate you!" She went to our parents. "Do you know what those dreadful boys are doing? Do you know what they're actually doing? They are digging a grave, my grave! Isn't that the most disgusting thing you've ever heard? Would you kindly talk to them? It's not very nice, what they are doing."

The grave was tolerated by our parents briefly, and then Dad filled it in. However, they, especially our mother, favored the boys and their bizarre sense of humor. The outline of the hole where the grave had been was still there ten years later when I searched for it, but the walls finally collapsed inward. The incident left Nancy with a permanent horror of death for the rest of her life.

Nancy occupied one of the two bedrooms at the front of the house. She had a four-poster bed with a hand-tied lace canopy on the frame. I envied her sleeping in that regal bed. When she got older, Nancy was so popular at dances that boys would form a long line on the dance floor waiting to cut in.

Phil and Ken had what they called "No Crying Fights," kicking, scratching, slugging each other but not uttering a sound for fear of adult recrimination. They insisted on being annoying: holding up two rabbit-ear fingers behind the head of especially elegant great-aunts, pretending to be cripples by dragging their legs on the street. When unsupervised at the dinner table they gargled milk, smacked their lips loudly, pretended to stab themselves in the stomach with their forks, played tag around the table. At other times they threatened Nancy and me with live worms.

But they had their good sides, too. Ken loved music and singing, and crooned Nat King Cole songs. He longed to be a drummer like Gene Krupa. Both boys played ice hockey, football, and rugby. He and Phil trained me to throw a spiral pass. They taught me how to skid my bike into a dramatic, gravel-spitting halt. They loved the Yankees, especially Joe DiMaggio and Mickey Mantle, so I did, too. They listened to "The Green Hornet" on the radio. I admired them and copied their boy behavior. I owned a football helmet, boxing gloves, and a punching bag.

Phil was ten years older than I. He had red hair and freckles and wore tortoise-shell eyeglasses. He insisted that he had taught me my first words. He swore that he spent hours sitting next to my crib and repeating out loud, "Phil knows best, Phil knows best," until I finally parroted him. When I was a slightly older baby, he pushed me around in a wheelbarrow. He was very proud of me and always teased me, which I hated. Now I think it was a rough and tumble way of showing affection, even the day before he died.

Ken looked like our father, with a handsome round face and dark hair. He was seven years older than I was and thin because he had asthma. He taught me to tie my shoes. He owned a pet chicken named Chicken during the War when we grew a Victory garden and raised chickens for food. Unfortunately, Chicken was eaten by a friend who misunderstood Ken's instructions for her care.

Ken had a sweetness but also a dark streak. One time when I was older he backed me up to a sturdy tree and tied my long braids tightly around it, then left me alone, helpless and afraid, in the woods, until he finally returned and freed me. (Probably I was alone for about five minutes, but it seemed like forever.)

The wooden house was painted a pale cream and had dark green shutters. Its front was surrounded by a porch, and some evenings we ate there in the oppressively humid Jersey heat. Sometimes the house seemed overwhelmed by the vegetation that surrounded it. On those nights my father and I took a swim before bedtime, threading our way down the hill on a dark path through an arborvitae grove and plunging into the barely visible water. The pool was fed by an icy stream and seemed even colder in the dark, with lightning bugs flashing.

Two large locust trees stood like sentinels in front of our house. In wintertime, Dad hung a large, oval silver-colored tray between the trees. He would shake sunflower seeds from a tin onto the tray for hungry cardinals, bluebirds, chickadees. Squirrels which lived in the trees learned how to teeter-totter like circus tightrope walkers along the wires that held the tray up, stealing the seeds or tipping the tray into wild gyrations, spilling everything onto the ground, including the marauding rodents themselves.

Inside our house, all of the rooms were small. Before I was born, two new little bedrooms for me and Yoyo were hammered to the back of the house on the second floor. The two new rooms were called the Norton Memorial Eyebrow, after a friend who donated them and helped to build them. When I was about six, I tumbled from one of the windows in the middle of the night, still asleep, landing on my face in the bayberry bush and breaking my nose. My parents woke up to the sound of someone crying and found their little girl outside, wandering in the dark, still asleep. Yoyo was gone that night, and I had sleepwalked out of the loose screen on her window. I don't have any memory of this at all.

The Big House

Indian War Hoop

Over the years I've received many comments that the page in Pat the Bunny *about "Daddy's scratchy face," with the sandpaper that represents his stubble, is one of the rare examples in children's books of something clearly oriented towards boys. Men wring my hand and seem very moved by the existence of this masculine item.*

Chapter Three: The Twenties and Early Thirties

The Crash

My Mother Writes Children's Books

My mother attended Bryn Mawr, the rigorously difficult women's college, and the Union Theological Seminary, where she met another student and fell in love with him. Her parents, Granny and Gampy, didn't approve of him and made her break off the engagement. My grandparents shipped their daughter off to Paris for a year with her maiden aunt, where she studied art at the Sorbonne and corresponded with my father, whom she had met at a house party before she left home.

Dad graduated from Harvard College in 1923 and Harvard Business School in 1925. My parents married the same year. My mother insisted that the word "obey" be omitted from the ceremony. A few years later they went to Leeds, England, with their toddlers Nancy and Phil, Jr. for my father to study his trade, the textile business. His father owned woolen mills in Lawrence, Massachusetts, and Dad had worked for his father ever since he was a schoolboy, learning spinning, weaving, dyeing, designing.

After they returned to the States, they lived in a small house on Mount Kemble Avenue at the bottom of the Hill. My father began his commuting life, taking the train every day into the city. He hated New York City with its congestion and crowds, and he preferred never to spend the night there. Soon they moved to the little Victorian house that they would rent for the next thirty-five years.

Eight years before I was born, in 1929, the Stock Market Crash took place. My paternal grandfather, George E. Kunhardt, whom we called Guppa, lost his textile mills and his 38-bedroom mansion. He ended up living in the gatehouse of his estate in North Andover, drinking. On Wall Street, men jumped out of skyscraper windows when they learned their stocks had been wiped out and their currency was worthless. Others were reduced to standing in lines for bowls of free soup because they had no money to buy food.

During the Great Depression, Dad was one of many out of a job. In 1931, he drove his family to Maine for the summer because groceries were cheaper there. He left my mother and Phil, Nancy and Ken on Ile au Haut, a lovely little island near the Canadian border, where they had friends. My mother had discovered she was pregnant again. Desperately worried about finances, she embarked on a home-remedy method, as several of her friends had done, to rid herself of their fourth child. She wrote to my father, "Last night I took ten grains of quinine and a very large dose of castor oil and a hot bath. Needless to say, I am not feeling very well today. I have just taken ten more grains of quinine, and am about to go and sit in a very hot tub." The long and ghastly process of causing an abortion made her sick, and could have killed her. However, she was finally successful. The incident haunts me.

The Great Depression lengthened and deepened, and the need for money grew because

Nancy and Phil would soon enter private school. (Free public school education was, to my parents, out of the question, as they felt the quality of education in public schools was poor.) My mother buckled down and wrote her first children's book in 1934, employing what she had learned in classes in child psychology and elementary education at Bryn Mawr and from observing her own children.

The first children's book division of a publishing company had been started at MacMillan in 1922, but "baby books," as they were disparagingly called, were still the ugly stepsister of publishing. However, in the 1930s, New York's Bureau of Educational Experiments, also known as Bank Street because it was located on Bank Street in Greenwich Village, became a respected center for research on childhood development as well as a functioning nursery school and a training ground for teachers.

The driving force behind Bank Street was its founder, Lucy Sprague Mitchell, whose primary goal was the documentation of language development, based on the discovery that children play with sounds long before they begin to use words, and that it is the child itself who is a wellspring of imagination.

Lucy Sprague Mitchell's discoveries led her to believe that traditional fairy tales did not necessarily constitute the best introduction to literature for the very young. Real things and experiences from a child's world were more suitable. This experimental theory became known as the "Here and Now" principle of progressive education. In order to immerse themselves in the Here and Now, Bank Street teachers took classes in art, music, dance, and pantomime, as did their young pupils. I've read that, after a visit to a dairy farm, the Bank Street School children were asked to act out the events of the day. When they reached one of the high points, milking, Lucy Sprague Mitchell herself offered to play the cow.

Countering Lucy Sprague Mitchell's ideas was Anne Carroll Moore, children's librarian at the New York Public Library and a proponent of traditional children's literature and education. A bitter debate raged for years between the two factions, and eventually drew in psychiatrists, psychologists, educators, and librarians on both sides.

My mother was well aware of the Bank Street experiments and innovations. She actually attended adult classes at Bank Street, and we still have one of her assignment papers, corrected by Lucy Sprague Mitchell.

The first book that my mother wrote and illustrated was *not* traditional. It was called *Junket is Nice*, and it was published by Harcourt Brace. For submission to the publisher, my mother prepared a dummy book, printing the words by hand and painting her illustrations with four colors. Harcourt Brace, after keeping her waiting for months because it took them time to work out the manufacturing problems that the book presented, finally accepted the story and illustrations, but planned only two colors, black and red, and sent her back home again to start over. My mother believed she could never execute the drawings as well a second time, so she threw the dummy book into a bathtub full of water. The colors washed off, and the dummy became inflated, but Harcourt Brace Publishers used the line art anyway for the finished book, and with only two colors besides black.

Junket is Nice had a distinctive shape, long horizontally, and, although there were pictures drawn in what would soon be known as my mother's inimitable style, the emphasis was equally on words. Words, printed in my mother's hand and not set in type, spilled and filled and dominated the left-hand page. In huge run-on sentences, like children's, and full of repetition, they dominated the book.

"Once there was an old old man with a red beard and red slippers. He was sitting at a table eating out of a big red bowl. He was eating junket out of the big red bowl. The old man ate and ate and ate. More junket and more junket and more junket and more junket until at last people began to be very much surprised at how much junket he was eating and they began to tell their friends about him because he seemed to be such a hungry old man. So people and their friends began coming to look at the old man eating his junket." Junket was a milk-based pudding, a jelled and sugary rennet product that we often ate with chocolate sprinkles. At my house, we loved it very much.

Soon all the people in the world surround the old man. The last to arrive is a little boy on his tricycle. At this point the book becomes a guessing game. The old man tells the people three things he's NOT thinking about: a walrus with an apple on its back, a one year old lion blowing out the candle on his lovely birthday cake, and a cow with her head in a bag, and all the people in the world decide to just guess everything else.

Among other guesses, they guess a pig seeing how many minutes it takes for a cold bath.

"WRONG! said the old man and he went on eating his junket."

They guess a deer with Christmas ornaments on his horns waiting around the corner to surprise Santa Claus.

They guess a vulture looking all around the rocks for five lumps of sugar, a rabbit wondering if there could be a bunch of grapes tied to his tail, and all of the guesses are WRONG!

In the end, the little boy on a tricycle guesses that the old man is thinking about ... "JUNKET!" The giant upper case word reaches across the centerfold of the book, creating an exclamation of humongous dimensions. As a reward, the boy gets to lick the bowl. Then he gives the old man a ride home on his tricycle. "And all the time that they were riding home to the old man's supper the old man said Oh my oh my oh my oh my oh my but JUNKET IS NICE!"

Franklin P. Adams, a famous columnist and reviewer at the time, wrote on the first page of the *New York Herald Tribune* Sunday Book Review, "Once there was a new, new book with a red jacket and a red cover, and a man who had on a blue shirt and a yellow tie saw the book with the red jacket and the red cover in a book store, so he went into the store and bought the book and took it to his white home that had three boys and one girl in it and two dogs and one cat. ...The boys said it was the best book that anybody ever wrote in the whole world and the country. RIGHT, said the man, who had read a million and a hundred books. I think that it is a book with the greatest sympathetic simplicity and the most poetic and affectionate imagination I ever saw, and I don't except *Little Black Sambo* or *Alice's Adventures in Wonderland.*"

In another review, the contents of the book were called, "Noble nonsense, that, like Lear's, could be at once ridiculous and poignant."

With *Junket Is Nice,* my mother had already become an innovator in the field of children's books, and went on to write 45 of them in all. She was a contemporary of Margaret Wise Brown, Ludwig Bemelmans, Dr. Seuss, and others, an extraordinary group of authors and artists from this extremely fertile period in children's literature. Franklin P. Adams took her to *The New Yorker* magazine Round Table meetings at the Algonquin Hotel. She said that Dorothy Parker was rude to her. I don't know why, except that I'm told that Dorothy Parker was rude to many people.

After the publication of *Junket Is Nice,* my mother's career blossomed. She wrote *Lucky Mrs. Ticklefeather* about a lady and her pet puffin, Paul, with whom she lives "in a high high terribly high building" in the city. Mrs. Ticklefeather and Paul play with blocks, model things out of clay, paint with an easel and brushes, and she dances an interpretive dance depicting a sunflower, which is Paul's favorite flower. When Paul is stolen, the old lady sends a policeman to search for him, and this book too becomes a guessing book.

Now Open the Box was about Little Peewee the Circus Dog. He was "the teeniest weeniest teeny teeny teeny weeny weeny weeny little dog in all the world." He didn't know any tricks, not even how to roll over, but he was so teeny weeny that everybody loved him. "But one day a terrible frightful awful thing happened. One day little teeny weeny weeny weeny Peewee started to grow."

"And he grew

"and he grew

"and he grew

"until poor little Peewee was just the same size as any other plain dog." The circus owner had to send him away because he couldn't even do any tricks. "So poor little Peewee started to go away and never come back to the circus any more and JUST THEN a wonderful splendid beautiful thing happened." He started to grow.

"And he grew

"and he grew

"and he grew

"and then the circus man said Oh my dearest little Peewee now you won't have to go after all because now you are so lovely and big!"

Now Open The Box was analyzed by Ellen Handler Spitz in *Inside Picture Books,* about the psychological aspects of some children's books: "When Peewee grows, he is no longer unique. He has become just like any ordinary dog. ...[so] he will be sent away. The scene, despite (and actually because of) the humor of its characters, is one of pathos. Manifestly straightforward, it taps directly into one of young people's deepest anxieties—the envy and fear of being replaced by a new love in the form of a newborn sibling.

"This apparently simple picture book, by using the pictorial device of amplifying its principal image page by page, conveys subtleties of psychological wisdom. Children who encounter it may come to understand, by means of projection and identification, that being lovable does not necessarily mean staying small (that is, refusing to progress or regressing in imitation of an envied infant or one's own former self). *Now Open the Box* implies...that, if children are to form stable, resilient selves, they must gradually and never without some pain relinquish the idolization of infancy and accept their growing bodies."

Another exceedingly popular book of my mother's would never, ever be published today, and it has also invited psychoanalysis. *Brave Mr. Buckingham* is about Billy, a boy who has climbed up high into a tree because he doesn't want to have his wiggly tooth pulled out. To calm him, his uncle tells him a story about an American Indian named Brave Mr. Buckingham.

"He was called Brave Mr. Buckingham because he was very, very, very brave. And Brave Mr. Buckingham had plenty of chances to be brave because so many terrible accidents happened to him. The reason Mr. Buckingham had so many accidents happen to him was that he spent his time doing foolish things, and doing foolish things is very dangerous. No matter how frightfully terrible an accident happened to him, Brave Mr. Buckingham just smiled a brave smile and said, 'THAT DIDN'T HURT!' (The terror of the situation is blunted by the fact that Mr.

Buckingham is made of NUGG, "and NUGG is a kind of stuff that is a little bit like clay and a little bit like iron and a little bit like wood and a little bit like rubber and a little bit like blotting paper.")

At the end of this audaciously funny book, Brave Mr. Buckingham—or all that remains of him, his head, after his limbs have been separated from him one by one—happily eats strawberries, fed to him by his granddaughter, and announces, 'THAT DIDN'T HURT!'"

This book is out of print, and it would never, never, never be published today because of its odd violence. My mother's great-grandchildren still love it, perhaps because the book addresses one of childhood's basic fears, that of losing body parts (even teeth that are loose and about to fall out), and yet at the end Mr. Buckingham, cheerful as ever, seems happy without them and still enjoys being alive. His cheerfulness certainly reflects the ethic of denial that was so strong in my childhood.

The choice for a main character of a Native American who is not quite human, doesn't have real blood or bones, and is named "Buck" might be seen today as unconscious racism.

As odd as this book is, I'm very fond of it. I think it contains my mother's best illustrations, especially her use of black in the art. To me, the black tree trunks and other elements resemble powerful inkblot images that seem to reveal psychological messages of rage and fear of loss beneath the amusing story elements.

← frog

back of the Hill

Pond with frogs + snakes

RING ROAD

soldiers

bark huts

grape vines — for swinging

horse chestnut tree

Nan's grave

pasture (skiing)

christmas Trees

stream

swing

sliding Hill

The Back Way

BARN Horses

ice HOUSE

MAI

THE HiLL ~ b

46

Log Cabin

jungle gym

gardens

greenhouse

BIG House

muffie's old house

...and Tony

stairs lived there

muffie's new house

trees

Anthony's accident

Sledding hill

muffie and Edith

My tree with the seat high up in the branches

Greenwood tree

thinking Hole

my father's garden

My father's shop-bees

Hair pin turns (steep)

ST

Forest

The FRONT WAY

icy cold pool

ROAD

Edith Kunhardt

Pat the Bunny has eight double-page spreads and is printed on shiny card stock. For many years it was the leader in U.S. children's book sales, and for decades it was second only to Beatrix Potter's Peter Rabbit in worldwide sales.

Chapter Four: The Forties, Part 2

Who Lived on the Hill?

The War

Every afternoon our landlady Bertha Jenks made her way from the Big House to a six-sided metal-lined wooden booth about twenty feet away. The box was just large enough to enclose a chair and someone sitting on it. She took off her clothes and sat naked inside for an hour. We children were urged to be quiet and play elsewhere at that time.

The box was an orgone accumulator. Orgone energy was discovered by a man named Wilhelm Reich in the 1930s. Reich claimed that orgone energy, or "primal cosmic energy," was responsible for the color of the sky, gravity, galaxies, weather, accelerated growth of plants, and orgasms, which were the release of orgone energy. Reich believed that the orgone accumulator gathered, concentrated, and heightened the energy, which radiated into a human's system from the air through skin and lungs and cured many medical conditions. The box was lined with alternating organic materials (to attract the energy) and metallic materials (to radiate the energy to the center of the box.) The energy itself was said to be manifested as a glowing blue aura around organisms, trees, and even mountain ranges. The Beat Generation novelists Jack Kerouac and William S. Burroughs found the effects of the accumulator to be curative and an aphrodisiac. Needless to say, the accumulator was very popular with patients and health practitioners. The user couldn't buy an accumulator in a store; it had to be ordered, or instructions could be obtained to make one. There were supplements to just the plain box. One follower even owned an orgone blanket.

The Food and Drug Administration disagreed with Reich about his invention, declaring that there was no such thing as orgone energy. The Administration burned the books he had written and tried to make sure that every book that contained the shocking word "orgone," so close to the unacceptable "orgasm," was destroyed. The Administration accused Reich of delivering misbranded and adulterated devices in interstate commerce as well as making false and misleading claims.

Today some people still believe in Reich's principals and denounce the FDA for burning his books. Some of his theories about sex, nature, and healing have gained acceptance. Orgone energy seems remarkably similar to our modern "Qi," prana, therapeutic touch, libido, feng shui, Several of Reich's books are back in print and people still hold seminars to discuss his work. Wilhelm Reich died in Federal prison in 1957, while serving two years for his unconventional beliefs.

Besides being a devout believer in orgone energy, Bertha Jenks was known as a great practical joker. Everyone in her family found her extremely funny. One evening, instead of raccoon, which was a favorite meat when food was scarce during the War, she served up a festive roast pet cat dinner. The dinner guests, when informed of the source of the meat (Bertha displayed the paws and tail) after they had happily devoured it, threw up. Bertha's family told that story with great hilarity for many years.

Bill Jenks, who was quiet and shy, loved taking his grandchildren on nature walks. He told them to bring along a shoebox, a ball of string, and a pair of scissors. The shoebox was to carry salamanders in, the string was to tie snapping turtles' jaws closed so they couldn't bite the children, and the scissors were to cut the string. Bill instructed the children never to turn a log over, exposing all the little wiggling creatures underneath, without turning it quickly back again so as not to unduly disturb the creatures' home.

Bill and Bertha had eight children, three of whom died untimely deaths, one from illness, one in a motorcycle crash, and another by shooting himself on purpose with his brother's gun. They were all buried in the family graveyard, which was at the top of the Hill in the woods.

When my parents and seven other families from the town founded a progressive school, Bill and Bertha generously donated the front half of the Big House for the schoolhouse and moved into the back half. My mother wrote about it: "Mr. Jenks has lent us his house on top of Mt. Kemble—given us every bit of it from the huge sunny rooms to the magnificent trees, and the feeling of far-up-in-the-heavenness. We should have come less splendidly near our objective had we not had these rare surroundings."

The school opened in 1929, the year of the stock market Crash. It was hard to raise money to start the venture. However, neighboring families were enthusiastic and generous. My parents donated $250, an enormous sum for the time. Soon they rounded up eight founding couples, and a teacher, who was paid. My mother wrote the first prospectus, which read, "Make each step in a child's education so absorbing to him that of his own impulse he is propelled from one undertaking to another. Let him so long to accomplish his task that time hastens by and he feels no weariness, only eagerness, and eventually satisfaction. Let all this happen and we have the high road to knowledge and the footpath to wisdom." My father was the first President of the Board. This private school had a kindergarten class of twelve pupils and added a new grade each year through seventh grade. It was patterned on the experimental, progressive, City and Country School in New York City, and run by Bank Street principles. The children studied Native American culture, building teepees in the woods, sewing birch bark moccasins and gathering sumac, which they boiled to make dye. They wore costumes and performed war dances. They studied storytelling, writing, painting, singing, dancing, and rhythms, which were skips and leaps, defined in the introductory materials as "peasant movements." The school was really a lab for the teachers, with the children as the subjects.

The students immersed themselves in the subjects being studied. For instance, when studying the Pilgrims, the students made candles in ancient molds and baked corn bread. To study the ancient Egyptian culture, they painted frescoes. To learn about the Vikings, they listened to *Die Walkure* and studied Norse myths. In a pageant, my brother Phil was the Aztec king, Montezuma, and wore a magnificent homemade robe. After a few years of operation on the Hill, the school moved to Bernardsville and finally to Far Hills. Today, now much less progressive and very popular, it is more than eighty years old.

After the school left, a new family consisting of two parents and two children moved in to the now-empty front half of the Big House. (Bill and Bertha remained in the back half.) The sister and brother with clouds of golden curly locks were only three and two. I was almost a year older than the girl and two years older than the boy. They were Beverly and Anthony, nicknamed Muffie (because her mother thought she looked like a muffin as a baby) and Tony, and they are still my friends.

We first met at the outdoor jungle gym, which had been built by Bill and Bertha to improve their children's health. It was a behemoth of a jungle gym, with many rings to swing on hand over hand, swings, poles to slide down, and a seesaw made of metal and painted silver. When the War began, Tony and Muffie's father, who was a lawyer, enlisted in the Navy and was put in charge of finding enemy submarines lurking off the shores of Long Island. Their mother was a nurse's aide at the local hospital, who, in her time off, sunbathed nude on the second-floor porch on the Big House and loved bird watching, horseback riding, and her flower garden.

When we were about seven or eight, we children were allowed to play alone in the woods on weekends and after school, and we always answered a shouted call for dinner. When we were really bored (there was no television then) we'd "Play a Story." Each of us thought up a plot, and then we voted, and whichever plot won was our game for the day. We played "Robin Hood," or circus, or rodeo, riding sticks, quirting ourselves on the flank as we galloped, and then roping and throwing steers and taming bucking broncos. We played pirates after seeing *Peter Pan* with Mary Martin on Broadway. We played Indians, taking pretend scalps from unsuspecting victims, or Superman, wearing flowing capes made of bath towels tied around our necks.

The Hill's own landmarks figured in our play—the Pool, the Upper and Lower Fields, the Apple Orchard, the private Graveyard that belonged to Bertha and Bill's family, the Pirate Ship (a ship-shaped island with two tall "masts" where two unpaved roads crossed), the Back of the Hill (full of swampy ponds with snakes), the Greenwood Tree (a gigantic pine whose fat lower branches grew almost vertically and which perfectly concealed Robin Hood and his Merry Men), and the Ring Road, which circled the top of the Hill. One winter Muffie and Tony and Cork, the Jenks' grandson, and I created an igloo out of a pile of snow that the snowplow had pushed up into a mound. After school we slid on trays on the steep, ice-slick fields and right into the ice house door for an abrupt stop on sawdust. Sometimes we drove electric cars that were stored in a barn. We mucked out stalls at the horse farm on The Hill and fed the horses grain and carrots.

When I played alone, I had other scenarios. I adored the British book series *Freddy the Detective* by Walter R. Brooks. Freddy was a talking pig who wore a deerstalker's hat and cleverly solved barnyard mysteries. Once Freddy dug a pit in which to capture someone, but the trap proved singularly unsuccessful, so he outfitted it with a mattress and used it for a "thinking hole." My thinking hole, minus the mattress, was in a forsythia bush.

My favorite place of all was a tall hemlock tree near my house. About twenty feet up, I found a place where two branches crossed, forming a comfortable seat, and spent hours there, hidden among the branches, watching the green pine needles dance in the breeze, concealing myself like a spy, listening in on people below, eating Mallomars, and reading books about Joan of Arc, which I hauled up by rope. I played alone a lot, especially after my brothers and Nancy went away to school. Sometimes I was lonely and sad, but I became expert at making up stories and entertaining myself.

During the War, Nancy was engaged to a soldier who was serving overseas. Phil was away at boarding school. Ken was kicked out of the same school for smoking and returned home for six weeks before returning. Ken taught me to squirm on my belly and crawl with my head down as pretend bullets whizzing overhead. My rifle was a real one, but a miniature, and it had a plug in the barrel. Ken shot squirrels with another rifle Dad owned. Dad also owned a German Luger, but he wasn't in the War because of his missing kidney.

One year I went to Muffie's birthday party in her family's half of the Big House. Downstairs, there was a trap door under the dining room table that concealed a tunnel-like space that had been used to store booze during the Prohibition. Upstairs, we played Murder in the Dark. There were squealing children in the bathroom, pushing against the door, and squealing children outside the bathroom, pulling on the door. I was helping Patricia, a schoolmate who was weak because she had infantile paralysis and wore braces on her legs. I was strong, and I muscled the door open just a crack. My little finger slid into the hinge part of the door. CRUNCH! The children slammed the door, and I screamed. My mother was in New York City, where she often was. Lib, one of Bertha and Bill's daughters, ran from house to house until she finally found a car that had gas in its tank; gas was rationed as well as food during the War. She drove me to the hospital, where they sewed on the tip of my finger that had been cut off by the door.

A quiet Japanese family lived in a cellar under Muffie and Tony's part of the Big House. The room was really a curing cellar, and there were hams wrapped up in butcher's paper hanging from the ceiling. Muffie and Tony used to punch the hams, which would swing wildly and the paper made a crackling noise.

The Japanese family consisted of Mr. and Mrs. Ohta, Arthur, their son, and Toshi, their daughter. "Father couldn't work," said Toshi when, decades later, I called to ask her about the Hill. She was in her late eighties and was married to Pete Seeger, the liberal activist folk singer, and was an activist herself.

In my mind, the "Japs" and torture and internment had nothing to do with the Ohtas. They were the most peaceful and helpful and distinguished family one could imagine. However, they were on guard, as the American Government had its eye on them because of the war. Whenever a strange car drove up the Hill's long, steep, winding driveway, the sound of its motor gave the Ohtas, who were usually working outside, time to run and hide in their curing cellar home. With Bill and Bertha's permission, the Ohtas planted vegetables such as cabbages, lettuces, and squash scattered among the day lilies, peonies, foxglove, poppies, and sweet peas in Bill and Bertha's flower beds, to disguise the fact that an extra family lived there and ate extra food. When she talked to me on the phone, Toshi insisted that she had only come out to the Hill from New York for fun, to play tennis, but later in our conversation, she told me more.

"He didn't go out much," she said about her father. "I was supporting the family by working at the 1939 World's Fair, but my father couldn't work because of the rules set up by the U.S. Government. He was detained under the Oriental Exclusion Act, which was passed by the United States Congress.

"We weren't as badly off as the other families of Japanese origin who lived out West." Out West, after the December 7, 1941, surprise attack by Japan on Pearl Harbor, hundreds of thousands of Japanese-American citizens in California, Oregon, Washington State, and Hawaii were taken from their homes by the U.S. Government and put in internment camps for the duration of the war, which lasted over four more years. They lived in tarpaper barracks without plumbing or cooking facilities. Often the families had to build the barracks themselves. At first they were not allowed to bring warm clothes for the winter even though the camps were in desolate places like Wyoming, where winter temperatures fell below zero.

"Even in the East, as Orientals we couldn't become citizens," Toshi continued. "My father was categorized as an Enemy Alien and was not allowed to travel. I was Stateless because I was born in Germany. Women didn't have many rights then, so I couldn't inherit citizenship from my mother, who was a U.S. citizen.

"People thought that 'Orientals' would stab them in their beds, so the police came and took away our knives and scissors. Have you ever eaten meat without using a knife?" Toshi asked.

Before the war ended, a fighting unit composed completely of loyal Japanese-Americans participated in the war in Europe and proved their patriotism by their fierce fighting and loss of life. Even so, some people believed "A Jap is a Jap is a Jap," meaning they were not to be trusted, ever.

Mr. Ohta himself had been horrified by the attack on Pearl Harbor. Muffie's mother found him sobbing as he cut out stars for Christmas decorations from gold paper and listened to the terrible news on the radio.

I recently spoke with Tony Mountain about the war. "At first Dad was stationed in Newark. He was in Naval Intelligence and was one of the people responsible for monitoring German submarines off the coast of Long Island. You know, U-boats actually surfaced there and German soldiers came on shore, where they were eventually captured. Dad was stationed in Newark for a year, and after that was elevated to Lieutenant Commander and transferred to Okinawa in the Pacific. There he worked on plans for the U.S. to invade Japan."

By then the country was weary of rationing, weary of death, weary of struggle, weary of war after four long years of fighting in Europe and in the Pacific. The plan was to blow up Tokyo Harbor and bring the whole long mess to a definitive end. A huge staff of people in Washington and Okinawa worked on the plan, but they were short on real, accurate information about Tokyo and its defenses.

One day in 1945, Tony's father, Worrall, was in his office in Okinawa when Mr. Ohta walked in. Worrall almost fell over with surprise, to see in this place the gentle man whom he had last laid eyes on and talked to so far away on our sheltered Hill in New Jersey.

Tony remembered, "Dad told me that Mr. Ohta said some things that made Dad ask him how he could possibly know them. That's when Mr. Ohta said he had just been in Tokyo. Dad was surprised—amazed—to hear that. Dad added that he knew that Mr. Ohta was a very strong American patriot and felt that Japan's decision to attack Pearl Harbor was a terrible and fatal mistake; Dad also knew that Mr. Ohta badly wanted to serve in the American Armed Forces but had had trouble getting into the Navy." Worrall speculated that Mr. Ohta must have joined the Navy by offering his services as an American spy in Japan. Tony remembered, "Dad never went into any particulars about what Mr. Ohta knew or said. It's a pity, because there must be a great story about how he got in and out of Japan and with whom he made contact."

The Americans didn't bomb Tokyo Harbor after all. President Truman decided to drop atomic bombs on the Japanese cities of Hiroshima and Nagasaki, killing half the population of each city, approximately 300,000 people in all. That ended the war with Japan.

Other people lived on the Hill for long or short periods of time. Elizabeth, or Lib for short, was the seventh of Bill and Bertha's children, and she lived in a cottage attached to the Big House. She was a sculptor, had been married to a U.S. Senator, and had one son. Lib was the first woman I knew who wore pants all the time, either plush corduroy pants, jodhpurs, or tailored twill trousers held up by beautiful belts with embossed silver buckles from the Southwest. She always wore well-polished Ferragamo shoes or boots. She was very stylish and worked at the fashion house Mainbocher in Manhattan. She had short grey-flecked black hair and, when on the Hill, packed a large 25-magnum Colt revolver in a holster on her belt, especially in the fall at deer-hunting time. She sternly warned off trespassers and informed them that the land was posted.

Lib's lover, a poet and journalist named Solita Solano, was originally named Sarah Wilkinson. Of course, as a child I didn't know that Lib and Solita were lovers or what that meant. I just knew that they took walks together, and that Solita wore gauzy pastel silks with lace at the collar and cuffs, and that Lib wore pants and smelled of cigarettes. Lib and

Solita met in 1943 when Solita was the partner of Janet Flanner, who was the Paris correspondent for *The New Yorker* magazine. Solita was friends with T.S. Eliot (whom she called "Tom") and Ernest Hemingway. While living with Lib on the Hill, Solita continued to work for Flanner as a secretary and editor. Solita had a fascinating face and was photographed by Berenice Abbott and Man Ray.

Janet Flanner was American but lived in France for long periods and won the National Book Award for Volume 1 of her book *Paris Journal*. She was awarded the French Legion of Honor in 1947 for her book *Letter from Paris*, edited by William Shawn. Flanner married a man but met Solita the same year, and the two started an affair. They were lifelong lovers, even though each of them became involved and lived with others during their relationship. Flanner's ex-husband was supportive of Flanner's career until his death. She wrote under the name Genet in her column, "Letter from Paris," and her writing became the epitome of *The New Yorker* magazine style: it was topical, elegant, funny, fresh, astute. She wrote her column for twenty years, with a break in the middle when she expatriated from France to New York during the war years and spent a lot of time on the Hill.

For the War Effort, we saved aluminum foil, which could be used over and over. Our parents were issued ration books that permitted us to buy a certain amount of butter or meat a week. Red stamp coupons were for meat, butter, fats, canned milk, and most cheeses. Blue stamps bought dried beans. One could also get shoes, coffee, and sugar with coupons. Gasoline for the car was rationed, too. An "A" coupon bought three gallons of gas, "B" and "C" coupons bought two half gallons. Phil and Ken collected 33 pounds and 16 pounds respectively of scrap rubber, for which they received 33 cents and 16 cents. When my mother really wanted a food item that she couldn't get legally, she went to Sweeney's, a store on Mt. Kemble Avenue that sold black market goods during the war. Sometimes we bought steak there, which we suspected wasn't steak but horse meat.

One day we bought a dozen eggs, and the next morning Mum cracked an egg open to cook it for breakfast, and we immediately began gagging when a disgusting smell arose. Inside the shell was an embryo chick, dead as a doornail and stinking to high heaven. I had to hold the egg in the car all the way back to Sweeney's, where it was exchanged for a good egg. Later we raised chickens of our own and grew a Victory

Garden near the house. I'll never forget my feelings of fear and disgust when a neighbor killed a chicken to eat and cut off its head. The blood spurted out of its neck as it hung upside down, twitching, its feet tied together with clothesline.

We sang songs popular during the War: "Mairzy Doats," "Oh, How I Hate to Get Up In the Morning," "Praise the Lord and Pass the Ammunition," "Anchors Aweigh." At night, we used blackout curtains to cover the windows when we had the lights on in our house, so that enemy planes would not see that we lived there.

Another frequent visitor to the Hill during the War, and a friend of Lib and Solita's, was the editor and publisher Margaret Anderson. With Jane Heap, Anderson had co-founded and co-edited an American literary magazine named *The Little Review* that became the most influential literary magazine in the world at that time. It was innovative because she introduced talented newcomers like Ezra Pound, William Butler Yeats, and T.S. Eliot to American readers. Anderson was discerning in whom she chose to publish. She once issued 64 blank pages between covers to protest the temporary lack of exciting new works.

Anderson's most important coup was that she serialized the first 13 chapters of James Joyce's *Ulysses* in *The Little Review*, the first time that any part of the book was published in America. This caused a huge stir, as the book was considered obscene. The co-editors were convicted of obscenity. At the trial two of the three judges slept through the testimony, a shocking symbol of judicial indifference. The judges roused themselves in time to convict Anderson and Heap, but the women didn't go to jail and only paid $100 each. In total, the U.S. Postal Service burned issues of the magazine four times.

Anderson met Dorothy Caruso, widow of the famous tenor, Enrico Caruso, on a boat when she was returning to the U.S in 1942 to evade the German occupation of France. The two became lovers. Whenever they visited, Muffie's parents complained that Caruso played wax recordings of her husband's arias extremely loudly, disturbing the tranquility of the Hill.

Anderson introduced the group of friends to the spiritual teacher and mystic G.I. Gurdjieff, and some of them became regulars in his intimate and prized special group that he called The Rope. Gurdjieff gave some of the members of The Rope nicknames. Solano was Kanari or

Canary, Anderson Yakina or a Tibetan yak, and Flanner was Camel. These names were deemed by Gurdjieff to enable each follower to enter her own "inner animal."

This close-knit group stayed in contact throughout their lives. Anderson's papers now reside in a collection named for Lib in the Bieneke Library at Yale. Flanner's and Solano's papers are together at the Library of Congress.

When the health of Lib's parents, Bill and Bertha, began to fail, Lib and Solita moved to the Hill from where they were living in France. After Lib's parents died, the two women moved permanently to Orgeval, France.

Farther down the Hill, at our house, Carl Sandburg used to come out from New York for the weekend to visit my parents. In one of my favorite photographs, Sandburg is teaching Muffie and Tony and me how to do the Indian war whoop at the Pool.

Sandburg was born near Chicago and dropped out of school when he was a youth. He delivered milk, harvested ice, laid bricks, threshed wheat, and shined shoes as well as became a hobo and rode the boxcars. When he was riding the rails, he learned many folk songs, and sang throughout his life. He became a famous poet and won the Pulitzer Prize twice, for his two-volume set *Abraham Lincoln: The War Years* and also for his *Complete Poems*.

My mother's father, whom I knew as Gampy, wrote a book with Sandburg, and my parents got to know him then. The collaboration came about because of my grandfather's collection of Civil War photographs.

Gampy's father, Major William Meserve, actually shook hands with President Lincoln when he was in the Union Army. The assembling of what later became the famous Meserve Collection of Civil War photographs began in 1897 when Gampy sought to illustrate William's war diary with photographs. His father was wounded twice in the Civil War, and he became a Major under General Burnside. He was a brave Union soldier who took part in the battle of Antietam. He wrote about the discomfort of marching, "My shoes gave out so that my feet touched the ground. This was not merely inconvenient but painful, but there was no help for it but to bandage my feet as best I could." He marched for many days in that condition.

By the turn of the twentieth century, Gampy's collection had mushroomed. Carl Sandburg wrote, "One day he called at the New York office of E. & H. T. Anthony and Company in Jersey City. That firm had in storage a collection of original portrait negatives made by Mathew B. Brady in his New York and Washington galleries. With a corps of assistants, Brady made the first extended series of photographs of a modern war."

What Gampy saw on the floor of that warehouse changed his life forever. He saw broken glass negatives, and intact ones. Some of them, he could tell, were taken by Matthew Brady, the famous wartime and battlefield photographer, and others were taken by Alexander Gardner, another Civil War photographer. Since Brady was bankrupt, my grandfather was able to buy on the spot 10,000 original Brady glass negatives, including seven previously undiscovered life negatives of Abraham Lincoln. This extraordinary find was a spur to further discoveries.

Soon several moving vans arrived at his home carrying the heavy negatives. It took workers hours to haul the load up to the fifth floor of his brownstone townhouse, and other boxes were stored in the basement. Cataloging and researching this tremendous haul took decades, and it was his life's work.

Gampy collaborated with Sandburg in writing *The Photographs of Abraham Lincoln,* published by Harcourt Brace. Sandburg paid tribute to his friend and co-author, writing, "...he became the acknowledged foremost authority on the photographs of Abraham Lincoln." The only existing print of a famous and powerful image of Lincoln that was made four days before his death but discarded because the glass negative was cracked, was one of his discoveries. The print is now in the Smithsonian's National Portrait Gallery. Gampy worked in the textile business, but his avocation was his collection, and he became the foremost collector of Civil War photographs outside of the Library of Congress.

My grandfather was born in Dover, Massachusetts, in 1865, the year that Abraham Lincoln was assassinated. The family moved to Colorado when Gampy was a boy, and he remembered standing on the last car of a train crossing the Western Plains and gazing at the dead buffalo carcasses which lay beside the tracks, while passengers beside him fired for sport into the brown backs of a gigantic herd of living, galloping animals that reached to the horizon. He also remembered, up until he died at 97 years old, the Morse Code that he had learned when he was nineteen, serving on the top of Pike's Peak year-round as a weather observer. He also became a hunter, an architect (he worked on the plans for the Antlers Hotel in Colorado Springs), a cowboy, a railroad surveyor, a map maker, and a city engineer. He held the record for the forty-mile walk, over a rough trail, from the town of Colorado Springs to the summit of Pike's Peak and back again in less than twelve hours.

Gampy and Granny got married when he was thirty-six years old and she was eighteen. They adored each other and lived together for over fifty years in their brownstone house on East 78th Street in Manhattan. Granny called it "The Manner House," because she insisted that the grandchildren learn on which side of one's dinner plate the fork went, never to put one's elbows on the table, never to talk with one's mouth full. As we grew older, naughtiness crept in; several of the grandchildren (including me) remember being caught by Granny smoking cigarettes in an upstairs room while spending the night. Neither Granny nor Gampy ever drank alcohol, but when Gampy found his wondrous cache of photographs of Lincoln, he later recalled, "I had my first experience of the sensation of intoxication...the only kind of I have ever experienced... that comes from the possession of a rare find."

My mother inherited her father's fascination with the Civil War period. She became a collector of memorabilia. In our house we had Mrs. Lincoln's traveling commode, hair from the tail of Mr. Lincoln's horse, a brick from Lincoln's home in Kentucky, a cast of Lincoln's hands, and the antique sperm-oil-burning lamps with cut-glass dangle shades, by the light of which the Lincolns were married.

Life went on in New Jersey. Nancy saw "Gone With the Wind" nineteen times. She collected Wendell Wilkie buttons. He was running for President, but he lost. She moved out of her room with the canopied bed, and I moved in.

Mum gave Dad a wheelbarrow for Christmas. She had a hard time getting it in the house and hiding it from him. He was almost as excited about the wheelbarrow as he had been when she gave him his own live honeybees, which arrived in the mail.

That same Christmas, Dad gave Mum amber. She loved amber in the form of bracelets, necklaces, or simply blobs of the smooth, glowing prehistoric tree sap. It was known to retain the heat of your body even though you weren't touching it anymore. Dad gave her amber every year, until she finally got thoroughly sick of it. She didn't want to hurt his feelings by admitting she couldn't stand it anymore, so she pretended to still like it. Eventually she told him she would like cash instead. Dad thought that was rather odd, in fact totally implausible, but he finally gave in, and I think she received fifty dollars.

Another Christmas we experimented with receiving only one present each. Ken got a hockey stick, Phil received an Oz book and Nancy got a pure gold pair of tiny scissors from Tiffany's for her charm bracelet. I got my tricycle. I rode around the house, calling out, "Toot, toot! Toot, toot!"

Dad couldn't restrict himself to the "one present rule," so he gave the family a tent as well as Lincoln Logs. He and Mum set the tent up in the living room and crawled inside, where they spent an hour, talking about how wonderful Eisenhower was as a President.

After the tremendous success of *Pat the Bunny,* my mother wrote and illustrated three other books in the same format, adding new ingenious moving parts. *The Telephone Book* had an attached cardboard telephone receiver and a wire made of string. This book featured Paul and Judy, and added a little brother, Timmy. The reader pulled up a cardboard blanket to cover

Timmy when he went to bed. *Tickle the Pig* featured Timmy's stuffed animal friends. *More, Please* was subtitled *The Hungry Animal Book.* It came with an attached box of paper food: a peanut, a piece of grass, a lump of sugar, a bone, a carrot, a fish, a worm, a piece of bread with jam, and a cookie. The reader fed the elephant, the cow, the horse, the dog, the rabbit, the seal, the bird, and the child through die-cut mouth openings in each page. The food fell down between the double pages and into another attached box.

LUCKY

MRS.

TICKLEFEATHER

by Dorothy Kunhardt

WISE OLD AARD-VARK

by
Dorothy Kunhardt

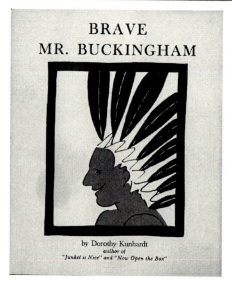

BRAVE
MR. BUCKINGHAM

by Dorothy Kunhardt
author of
"Junket is Nice" and "Now Open the Box"

My status as the first "reader" of Pat the Bunny *makes me a minor celebrity in this "bunny eat bunny world," which some people call children's book publishing. I have been interviewed by the* New York Times, *featured on the cover of* Publishers Weekly, *interviewed on* National Public Radio, *and I appeared with a live rabbit perched on my shoulder in* People Magazine *on the 50th anniversary of the book's publication.*

Chapter Five: The Forties, Part 3

My Mother and Our Treats

I spent a lot of time with my mother because my siblings were away at school and my father was working. Yoyo wasn't there all the time. Before I started kindergarten, I often went shopping with Mum. We would drive the three miles from our house. On the way she would help turtles who were in danger of being run over across the road. We loved the shoe store in Morristown, because it had a machine which Xrayed our feet. That was supposed to help us find the right shoe size. I remember peering down at the bones in my feet displayed in ghostly exposure and wiggling my toes. Years later, it was discovered that too many X-rays could give you cancer. We picked up groceries at Foster's Market. Mum got a permanent wave while I read movie magazines, and then we went to Day's Soda Fountain for a hot fudge sundae.

The school that my parents helped to start had a wonderful faculty, especially the French art teacher, Madame Wadlow, whose guidance led to six out of ten of my classmates, including myself, becoming professional artists or illustrators. The other teacher who inspired us was an English teacher named Mrs. Noling. When I saw her fifty years later, she quoted from my story about a mole: "'Be eyes for me,' said the baby mole" was the part she especially liked. My story, called "Mole Meets a Frieind" (sic), was imaginative and strong but full of spelling errors and non sequiturs. I still have it and the homemade book in which it appeared.

At a summer workshop, my friend Muffie and I made our own books, sewing the binding, painting the illustrations, decorating the cover with flowers and vines. I wrote a story about Rosie, the hippopotamus in the Central Park Zoo.

"She had a pig's tail," I wrote, "and tiny little muddy eyes on two raised bumps. Her shiny purple skin was hard and stretched smooth over her big, round body."

After I transferred in fourth grade to the Peck School in Morristown, my mother sometimes wrote stories or assignments for me, and I unfailingly passed them off as my own. She wrote for all of us children and sometimes for my father, who had to produce reports for his volunteer work at the local hospital and the Community Chest. We were immensely proud of her for her prowess in taking on our voices. My parents were worried about me at this time and they had my IQ tested. The results showed I was intelligent, yet lazy and careless. Was this dyslexia, which was practically unknown then? Or boredom?

Here is a story my mother wrote for me when I was about 10. She had a remarkable knack of getting right into a child's mind.

"My mother asked me the dreaded question. 'Do you want to go to Dancing School this Fall?'

"The answer was, of course, 'No!' For there rose before my eyes visions of small boys coming up to my waist, dancing with me, their little hot hands clutching at my back, and their big, heavy feet crunching my toes.

"There also arose in my mind the horrible thought that I had just had a birthday.

"The first thing that Mr. Merrylegs, the Dance Master, would do was call out the names of some of those people who had had birthdays recently.

"Then some poor victim would have to get up and dance with me, while I turned a deep, beautiful purple.

"So I gave up the opportunity to go to Dancing School this year, and accepted the opportunity to have riding lessons. I would rather dance with a horse than with the supply of pigmy partners awaiting me in Dancing School."

I happily read the story aloud to the school assembly, taking credit as its author, and was applauded enthusiastically. It was published in Peck School's *The Wood Pecker*, and with each accolade I swelled with pride and continued to accept my mother's help. Deep down in the bottom of my heart I thought this might be wrong, but I wanted the praise, so I perpetuated the lie. Mum didn't always write my essays and never laid eyes on my arithmetic homework; I suspect she was bad at math herself. I don't know why the school did not seem to notice that my mother was doing my homework. Was it her formidable personality that threw them off the scent?

Another story I passed off as my own was an account about waking up at dawn to hear the radiators in our house banging like drums, and my father's loud snoring turning into horse-like snorts. The assembled students found it hilarious. Another story was about New York busses "with their wide rubber lips."

Mum used vivid descriptive phrases and sophisticated vocabulary, whereas my writing style was quieter and I didn't employ exaggeration as much for humorous effect. Sometimes an essay she wrote or helped me with was about Abraham Lincoln, which was not my favorite topic, but because my mother was a Lincoln scholar, she fed me ideas. With her help, I wrote about "Mr. Lincoln's Public Opinion Baths," which described the habit President Lincoln had of periodically allowing any and all citizens into the White House and into his presence to complain, criticize, and cajole.

I was featured in a newspaper story about Lincoln in the *Newark Evening News* when I was ten. The local library was exhibiting the original casts of Abe's hands that came from her father's

Collection. The plaster casts illustrated that Abe's right hand was swollen from shaking hands with hundreds of neighbors who crowded into his house to congratulate him on winning the Presidency. Also there was a life mask in the exhibition, and an article described how plaster was applied to Abe's face to make the cast. He had to sit absolutely still for the hour it took to harden. Bits of his eyebrows came off when the plaster was removed.

Having my mother write some of my assignments didn't seem wrong, just an affirmation that she was the writer, one of steely and proud invincibility and a rigid grasp of grammar. Once, many years later, when I was a children's book editor, I asked her if she and I could write something together. Her facial expression of extreme scorn silently conveyed her answer.

The most popular girl's game in seventh grade was Jacks, along with Canasta. We girls sat on the locker room floor between classes, scooping up jacks and tossing them out again. I remember getting splinters under my fingernails from scraping up the little objects up from the wooden floor. It was also the year of card games. We even played Canasta over the phone. The three boys in our class were not interested in Jacks or Canasta.

At about that time, I developed a temper, especially when things didn't go my way. For instance, sometimes when I wore a dress with a zipper, the zip got caught in the lining and became completely stuck. I made things worse by getting furious and trying to rip the dress apart. Sometimes I succeeded.

Nancy was heartbroken when my mother insisted that she break her engagement to her soldier friend. Mum didn't seem to remember that Granny and Gampy had done the same thing to her. Nancy saved the soldier's letters for the rest of her life, even though she fell in love and married someone else and they had six children.

Nancy got married when I was ten. To pay for her wedding, my mother wrote twenty-four little books, just the right size for a child to hold in her hand. Twelve of the books were "Nonsense Stories," imagined tales about animals dressed up and behaving as people would. Twelve of the books were about animals in their natural habitat with very authentic animal behavior. The books were popular, filled as they were with my mother's sharply humorous and astute observations of children, animals, and families. Garth Williams, the illustrator of E.B. White's *Stuart Little*, Laura Ingalls Wilder's *The Little House on the Prairie*, and Margaret Wise Brown's *Little Fur Family*, did the charming paintings. One little book, called *The Naughty Little Guest*, was about Margaret, who invited her imaginary friend, Estelle, over to her house. "Play nicely, now, children," Mrs. Goat said, but Estelle did not play nicely. She refused to pull Margaret in the wagon. She splashed water on Margaret's dress. She drew a picture on the living room wall. Finally Mrs. Goat called Estelle's mother and sent Estelle home.

At school we had organized sports, like soccer and field hockey. I remember that the opposing team always shouted, "Peck, Peck, Stinks Like Heck!" My mother came to all my games. She had played field hockey at school and was on the water polo team at college, and yet I never saw her in shorts or in a bathing suit my whole life. She always wore a dress. She also wore stockings and shoes, except on the hottest days when she put on sneakers and left her legs bare. Her only makeup was a little lipstick; she wasn't interested in wearing nail polish or dyeing her hair or reading fashion magazines.

In the fall, which was football season, my parents and I always went to see my brothers at their boarding school in Massachusetts. It was a seven-hour drive. Nancy was at high school in New York and during the school year, living with Granny and Gampy, so she didn't go on these trips.

I liked being in the car with Mum and Dad. When I was four or five, we had had a car named Chowdog with an enclosed front seat and an open rumble seat. When I was older I lay on a little shelf behind my parents in the enclosed front seat. I fit onto the shelf perfectly. It was fun to be quiet and listen to them talking. It was fun to look out at the world from their eye level.

Now we had a car with an enclosed front and back seat and no name and no rumble seat. I usually rode in the back seat. There were no seatbelts, of course. We had a game. We would point out landmarks along the road. Here was the bridge that made a humming sound when the car passed over it. Could I hum all the way across? Here the road curved to avoid a famous oak tree that was known far and wide. Here we recited in unison the rhymes from the Burma Shave signs: "Passing cars/ when you can't see/ may get you a glimpse/ of eternity/ Burma Shave." Or "The draftee/ tried a tube/ and purred/ Well whaddya know/ I've been defurred/ Burma Shave." We stopped at favorite roadside restaurants where the waiters knew us from previous trips and brought me extra little cellophane packets of nuggety Saltine oyster crackers to eat with my soup.

On the long drive home at the end of the weekend, I would get sleepy. I watched the darkness fall and the headlights of the oncoming cars flick on. I put my head on my father's thigh and my feet in my mother's lap. I listened drowsily to their conversation, looking up past the gear shift at the glowing phosphorescent dials on the dashboard. It would begin to rain, and Dad turned on the windshield wipers. The wipers clicked and swished hypnotically across the windshield. There would be a sound of rushing air and the purring of the engine. And I would feel completely safe and protected, speeding through the night.

In the eighth grade, when I got my first diary, I was still playing in the woods. I wrote, "There is no proof but Muffie and I suspect Tony and Cork of taking the rope ladder and collapsing Muff's hut, cutting my bow-string, and unsticking the ring from the rope." My new diary reported something else. At a party, "we started to square-dance but then played Spin the Bottle.

Greg, Page, James, David, Malcolm, Peter, and some other jerks kissed me. I hoped Mum wouldn't find out about Spin the Bottle but she did. Mrs. Hilton told Mrs. Mountain and Mrs. Mountain told Mum. I confessed and she already knew. It was awful!" I erased the following: "I was very surprised the way their lips felt—like people's lips. Just little boy lips."

My mother started to get on my nerves. She was always telling me to smooth my hair, stand up straight, and she was a perfectionist about my clothes. We often squabbled. At this time I started biting my fingernails more than usual, sometimes so much that my cuticles bled, and my natural outgoing style changed to shyness.

I got my period when I was thirteen. I was too bashful to call it "my period," so I dubbed it what my mother and sister called it: "The Curse." I didn't grasp that it could be seen as a natural event, a rite of passage. I don't remember what my mother told me about it. My female classmates and I compared notes: "Have you got it yet?" So I must have at least felt anticipation. Yet I remember anxiety, disgust, and fear that my body was bleeding. Later, as an adult, I discovered my mother had suffered from a similar ignorance of menstruation. She wrote, "I noticed a slight brown stain in my starched white pants that were held up by innumerable large buttons. In great embarrassment I went to my mother because I thought I had a dread disease. She looked, I thought, angry, marched to her bedroom bureau, returned with a pile of thick cotton 'Birdseye' babies diapers and a narrow waistband, two safety pins, said, 'Here, wear one of these. This will happen every month. It has to do with having babies.' I was in terror for years because I thought I was having a baby." I didn't think I was having a baby—I probably didn't get the connection—but I was obsessed with how to manage disposal, how to keep a ladylike appearance, and comfort: especially bothersome was riding a horse.

My mother often took me out of school, usually on Wednesdays when there were theater matinees on Broadway. (She arranged individual treats with my siblings, too. She believed time alone with each child was essential.) We took the train to Hoboken, then the Tube under the Hudson, then the subway up to 42nd Street. First, we always went to the Automat. I put nickels in the slot and little windows popped up, revealing a turkey sandwich, a slice of lemon meringue pie, or even a hot dish. We always had rice pudding for dessert. After that, we went to

Radio City Music Hall. We always sat in the front row near the orchestra pit. When the orchestra rose majestically from the depths, we waved to our special friends, the drummers and cymbalists and other percussion players. Sometimes the Rockettes kicked in unison on a ramp protruding into the audience. After that, they would take their places in lighted alcoves up and down the sides of the huge theater. A master of ceremonies with a gilt top hat and a cane would introduce acts. When the stage show ended, an organist played the brightly lit and colorful organ, making our brains reverberate in the low notes. Then we gathered our coats, ran to the stairs, and climbed up one, two, three tiers to take seats in one of the highest balconies to watch the movie on the giant screen.

We also went to plays on Broadway. We saw the original *The King and I* with Yul Brenner and Gertrude Lawrence, the original *South Pacific* with Mary Martin and Ezio Pinza, the original *Member of the Wedding* with Julie Harris and Ethel Waters, and many more.

When we were tired from our exciting day, we retraced our steps to the subway, the Tube, and the Hoboken Station, where we'd have some grape juice at a counter and go to the bathroom where the toilet seats were lit with phosphorescent lights to sterilize them. Finally, we took the Lackawanna train with its wicker seats back to Morristown.

At other times we visited the rodeo or the circus at Madison Square Garden. There she bought me a reproduction of the Giant's Ring or a whip or fake leather chaps. It didn't really matter where we went, although my mother especially liked the circus. The important thing was that it was our time together.

Our treats came to an end in the fall of 1951, when I was fourteen and went away to a girl's boarding school.

I knew Pat the Bunny *had become a cultural icon when a* New Yorker *magazine cartoon appeared. A teacher sits with her kindergarten class of very young children, whose diminutive chairs form a semi-circle in front of her. They have serious, expectant expressions and hold copies of* Pat the Bunny *on their laps. The teacher urges earnestly, "Please turn now to 'Judy's Mirror' in your copy of* Pat the Bunny*."*

Chapter Six: The Fifties

Away at School

I was busy for weeks before leaving for school, shopping for clothes with my mother. The girls at the school didn't wear uniforms, but we all dressed alike in yellow sweaters and gray skirts. We wore Abercrombie shoes with fringed tongues or Pappagallo flats, and polo coats. No jewelry was allowed. One of my roommates threaded strings through her pierced earlobes to keep the holes from closing up. She would again don her earrings when vacation rolled along. At school, I practiced standing up when an adult came into the room and holding the door for "Old Girls."

I adored my four years at the school and made lifelong friends. Highlights of my education were dissecting a fetal pig in Biology class, studying Henry James, and becoming permanently smitten by the history of art, taught by yet another wonderful teacher. I didn't receive the best grades, but neither of my parents ever told me that I should do better. They were proud of my accomplishments.

We were not allowed to leave the school except for rare occasions, and so we became very close to our classmates. The school traditions, songs, memories, challenges, and friendships deeply enriched my life and continue to do so today.

In my sophomore year, my first cousin, Pam, who also attended the school, went to visit her roommate in the Adirondacks and drowned in a nearby river. My mother wrote about the tragedy: "Forty men were roped together to search under the falls, but the rush of water was too strong. They finally had to put sandbags at the falls to divert the current. They found her under a rock which had beneath it a ten-foot deep whirlpool which no one had known was there. The falls have since been dynamited. Pam, after being swept over, never had a chance, strong swimmer though she was." I was horrified that my beloved playmate was gone. I wrote her mother letter after letter, and learned later that she never read any of them because it hurt too much. Pam's father's pain was so great that he refused to see her body and stood alone on the sidewalk outside at the funeral.

At the funeral home, I too hung back from seeing the corpse, but my mother grasped my arm in an iron grip and forced me into the room. A single line of liquid, somewhat like a tear, ran down from the side of Pam's closed eye, ending up in the sickly sweet-smelling flowers resting on her neck. I took a few blossoms and pressed them in my diary, not parting with them for many decades.

My senior year, I was elected Head of the School by my peers, which meant that I had to give a speech on graduation day. This was the greatest challenge I had ever experienced. All my shyness and low self-esteem rose to the surface. How could I speak in front of 200 people? How could I write a speech worthy of the honor of representing my class?

Naturally, I turned to my mother. I knew she would help me out; she always had. I was sure I couldn't write anything good enough. In fact, I had no ideas at all. I begged her to help me, and she responded to my plea.

I memorized the speech that my mother wrote for me and delivered it on Graduation Day. Part of the speech was about my progressive education in grammar school, and made the point that "educators sometimes allow students to go through make-believe experiences, resembling those they would meet later on in real life.

"There was a school near us in New Jersey where the program for third graders was an entire year of Indian life, designed to teach everything from resourcefulness to arithmetic. In June, a friend of mine, Arthur, brought home a report card that told of absolute failure, in everything, and his mother was desperate. Arthur constantly mislaid his wampum, so could do very little trading. He seemed to have no aptitude for corn grinding, his drumming was unsatisfactory, his war dance was spiritless. In artwork he had shown a tendency to copy the other children's buffaloes. His birch-bark moccasins were very inferior and had come unsewn immediately. And finally, no girl in the class was willing to be his squaw, and Arthur had to live alone, mournfully, in his lopsided, leaky, carelessly constructed wigwam. When his mother and old nurse, Delia, at their lowest moment of discouragement, had sat silent a long time, Delia said suddenly, 'But Mrs. Stewart, Arthur isn't going to *be* an Indian, is he?'"

Humor was followed by serious ideas such as, "We cannot even imagine what lies ahead, as we leave the quiet beauty of this countryside, knowing that atomic bombs are being exploded, and hydrogen bombs kept in waiting, while men and women work against time to find a way by which nations can live together as friends, and not destroy each other. Soon we will be the generation that will be responsible, and accountable, and it will be our part to translate our thoughts and beliefs into action. It may very well be that one thing we have learned here, seemingly a very simple thing, will prove to be the most valuable talisman we take away with us.... The ability to meet and work with people with the immediate attitude of liking them and wanting to understand them, does not sound like something that will change the world. But it still may, because nations are only vast multiplications of people like ourselves.

"We know that in taking this gift with us, the more through life we give it away, the more it will remain with us. There can be no end to such a power—that has its beginning in humble and grateful hearts, in this church today."

Amid all the people who crowded around to congratulate me after I spoke, one man faced me square and grimly accused, "You didn't write that speech, did you? It was too good!" He leaned closer. "Your mother wrote it, didn't she?"

"No!" I burst out, and wrenched myself away. That moment was to haunt me for thirty years, a source of deep shame, negating my love for the school and all the successes I'd had there. Release came years later when I visited the school and gave a talk there about my own career as a children's book editor and author. After that, the shame abated.

At college I majored in history of art. Learning about art made me feel like a citizen of the world, and enhanced my foreign travels later. There were no more bogus stories from my mother.

During my freshman year at college, my mother worried about my complexion and sent me to a dermatologist in the college town. I hated going to him. I was ashamed of having someone operate on my pimples, and I never told anyone where I was going for my mysterious appointment. The doctor's fingers were puffy and slightly sweaty. He worked away with a cold instrument on small zits on my upper chest, and also with his fingers, which perilously strayed over my skin toward my bra strap. I screeched "Stop!" inside my head, but the screech didn't get out. I never mentioned my dread and disgust to anyone. Dad was paying, and I didn't want to hurt his feelings.

I started smoking as a college student and gave up athletics. I smoked heavily for the next twenty years.

When I was a junior at college, my mother invited me to her women's club in New York to hear the Danish author Isak Dinesen read from her book *Out of Africa*, so I traveled up from Philadelphia. On the day of the talk I arrived in the elegant club library in a state of high excitement. "Go on, Dithie. Get closer," my mother whispered, poking me. I settled myself on the floor close to Ms. Dinesen's knee and stared up with wonder at the venerable author. She was ill and thin and suffering from advanced syphilis that she had unknowingly contracted from her husband. It was rumored that all she ate and drank were oysters and champagne. She wore a fluffy animal fur around her neck on that hot day and had deep, sunken eyes and a hawk-like nose. She wore a black hat with a wide brim.

She spoke fluent English in a deep, resonant voice with a melodic Danish accent. "I have been in the United States before, twenty-five years ago, when I came across the ocean in the shape of a book," she said. She meant *Seven Gothic Tales,* a great favorite in the American market. "I want to thank my American readers for their overwhelming kindness. My story is called 'The King's Letter' or, in Swahili, 'Barua a Soldani.'"

She started to speak instead of read, having committed her writing to memory. "On a New Year's morning, early in the morning while the stars were still hanging like clear drops in the sky, and while the African air, dry in the daytime, had in it that strange quality of liquidity, making one feel that one was driving along at the bottom of a deep, clear, sombre sea. I was driving on a very bad road through the Masai reserve with my English friend Denys Fitch-Hatton...."

Back at school, my college classmates and I constructed a sexy puppet Elvis Presley and danced with it, or at least, did some pelvic tilts.

On spring vacation, I noted that my parents now had separate beds. The house was becoming stuffed with old nineteenth century books, and my father's bed had become overrun by them, so he moved into Phil and Ken's old room. The books, all of which my mother read, bristled with her notes. Piles of them lay on the staircases, forcing one to dance one's way up, stepping into little clearings on the treads. Books rose high enough to block out cool night air from flowing in the bedroom windows.

Mum got the bulk of her books from a second-hand store in a poor part of town nicknamed the Hollow. "What have you got today?" she asked of the bent old man who stood by a ramshackle desk. He wore a large cardigan sweater around his thin shoulders. Secretly, I didn't like him much. He had a strange raspy voice and he spat when he talked.

Mr. Turitz was smart. He knew a thing or two about books. But so did my mother. They played the game of trying to trick each other out of gems from someone's estate. "This batch came in today," Mr Turitz would rasp, casually turning away. "Look 'em over."

My mother would leaf quickly through the books, studying copyright dates and quality of engravings and whether there was mildew on the pages. She liked old books about dead people in seances, civil war soldiers, prisons, circus freaks, old toys, railroads, animals, children, assassinations. Swiftly she'd make her choice, gather up an armful of books, and take them to Mr. Turitz.

"Four dolla," Mr. Turitz would say, scratching his armpit under his cardigan with long, dirty fingernails and spraying a fine mist of spit as he talked.

"What? These old things?" my mother asked, dismissingly "You know you were going to throw them away. All of them together are worth two dollars, at most," my mother would counter.

"You've got seven there. Three-fifty. Last offer."

"All right, but it's a crime."

Sometimes my mother made a bigger purchase. She wrote, "Yesterday I bought a stuffed crow at Turitz's as a surprise for Dad, and he certainly was surprised. I know people think I'm crazy, with my frequent visits to that old dusty second-hand book shop, and the crow would be convincing proof if anyone had happened to snap a photo of me yesterday. I exited briskly from the door of the shop and entered my car with a great black bird – beak half open, wings outstretched – in my hand. It really looks so alive its wings seem to be flapping. Dad thinks it was somebody's pet. I got it for a quarter and it was well worth it."

Dad suffered from depression in the Fifties. The textile industry was failing. Many weaving plants had moved to the South, where there was cheaper labor and no unions. Dad remained at a job he despised. Both my mother and father began to drink more and argue more. I remember them yelling at each other, and sometimes the car would roar away with a rattle of driveway gravel, not returning until the driver had calmed down.

It was about this time that I began to be ashamed of my parents. My mother was writing a new series about occupations, and part of the research she had devised for herself was to ride in the high cab of the garbage truck with the garbage man. This seemed terribly embarrassing. She also visited a barbers' school to watch the fledging barbers slather shaving soap on inflated balloons and then shave them, hoping they wouldn't pop. I just wanted her to be like all the other mothers and stop being so different!

My father was also a source of shame. The fact that he wasn't rich like many parents of the children in my private schools was humiliating, I thought, in my selfish way. I had no concept of the many sacrifices my parents had made for me to go to boarding school and take riding lessons. Something I would never admit to my friends was that Dad cleaned the house on weekends, while wearing his usual costume of Khaki shorts.

My father's health continued to deteriorate. He had a knee operation and wore a clumsy brace on his leg. The brace was hinged and squeaked when he walked. He had a hemorrhage and was carted off to the hospital. Next, his only kidney began to fail. There was not much his doctor could do to help this condition; dialysis was only a dream.

My mother's deeply etched frown became permanent, and the impatient tapping of her thumb on the car's steering wheel became a regular habit. She was extremely worried about Dad. Even though they continued to squabble, their bond remained strong, and she was his greatest and most devoted support as he continued to deteriorate.

She continued to support my life as a debutante.

"I drove in to N.Y. yesterday with all of Dith's evening dresses for three dances on Long Island -- Monday, Tuesday, Wednesday – and her suitcase full of bathing suits and other clothes for a three-day visit on Long Island. She is staying at the August Belmont's in Syosset and goes to a dance at the Piping Rock Club tonight."

I met my husband-to-be not at a dance but at a house party after the Harvard-Yale football game. It was November of my senior year at college. Ned was a nice, "preppy" man who went to the Right Schools, had served in the Army in Germany, and was finishing Harvard Law School. He had a benign, kindly expression and his eyeglasses made him look vulnerable. He seemed very kind but sometimes had a steely practicality. His idea of a test of character was, "If there was a house fire and your children and you were caught in it, whom would you rescue?" The "right" answer was yourself, as you are the repository for the knowledge which you have acquired over the years and which might benefit mankind. My answer was, "The children!" but that was the "wrong" answer. However, I was dazzled by his mention of the children that we might have. This blinded me to the harshness of the test.

We fell in love fast, even though we hardly knew each other and drank too much when we were together. He was in Massachusetts and I in Pennsylvania, but we saw each other as much as we could, wrote voluminous letters, made phone calls. I was well aware that I required a husband, and soon. After all, the only choice of career for a woman at the time was teaching or being a secretary. Of course, Ned came to visit the Hill, and we walked the circuit: the Greenwood Tree, the Pool, the Big House, Muffie, who had just gotten engaged, too, and my parents. He invited me to his family's farm in Connecticut, where there was a working Aga stove in the kitchen, identical to my family's Aga. His parents welcomed me warmly. What a coincidence: his mother, Lavinia, wrote children's books, and I had read some them in my horse-crazy stage! Ned had five brothers and sisters whom I immediately loved. It was one of those "marriages made in heaven," and I was very happy.

We chose a Saturday in November for the wedding.

"Oh, no, Mrs. Kunhardt!" the church secretary protested to my mother. "That's the day of the Harvard-Yale game, and no one will come!"

We meekly changed the date.

My mother, grandmother, and aunt took me to Bergdorf's to get lingerie for the wedding night and honeymoon. As they fussed over me and made me try on gauzy underthings, I was purple with embarrassment.

November 19, 1959, was my last night in our house on the Hill. I couldn't wait to get away.

Scribners Window

Chapter Seven: The Sixties and Seventies

Her Later Work

The Rest of Our Story

In fact, I went to bed on that last night in New Jersey with mixed feelings. I knew I'd miss my parents, but I couldn't wait to escape from them and the Hill, both of which had become oppressive and boring. Although I pretended to be calm about the wedding, I was really terrified of being the center of attention, while another part of me reveled in playing the part of bride. I wore my mother's wedding dress, which was a cloud of cream-colored satin and lace, with an impossibly nipped-in waist and a long train.

On the day of the wedding, I was a bundle of nerves. I was staying at Granny and Gampy's house on East 78th Street. Gampy was too frail to go to the wedding and reception. I was scared about the ceremony, and my nervousness increased when I talked to Ned on the phone. He was maddeningly calm, sure, and collected. He planned to get his hair cut and his shoes polished, mundane things that grated against my panic. We weren't allowed to see each other on the day of the wedding, which was a tradition that I didn't understand. I wanted to see him, badly. I had come to depend on him. My self-consciousness was increased by a pounding headache from all the drinks I'd had the night before. I flounced into the bathroom and slammed the door, making everyone worried for my sanity. It was plain old acting out—my sister did it all the time, but I didn't.

The actual wedding went well. My mother almost fainted at the reception because she had thought I was backing out at the last minute with my bathroom histrionics. She had worked herself to the bone to make my wedding and my wedding presents and the accompanying parties perfect.

We moved into a one-bedroom apartment on 89th Street and York Avenue on the Upper East Side. It was a pleasant neighborhood but slightly scruffy. I was twenty-two and Ned was twenty-seven, and having our own apartment felt very adult, at least to me. Ned seemed to be a grown-up, but I was still a child, acting the part of an adult.

I appreciated his mature outlook and worldly point of view. He had served in the Army in Germany as an officer, and he was a Democrat. He knew about foreign affairs and presidential politics. And he could drive a tractor. He owned a car. I liked Ike but really had no knowledge of politics, except that Eisenhower seemed like a nice old man. I had never voted.

However, we got along well, although I was dismayed that he worked so hard; he was an associate at a top law firm in Manhattan and left early in the morning, returning at about 11 p.m. almost every night. I really hadn't expected that in my dreams of the future. I wandered through a park next to the East River, sometimes with sketching materials, sometimes with a book. The days dragged. I didn't know how to handle the solitude.

At first I didn't even try to get a job. It was the end of the Fifties and the start of the Sixties and a girl with my background didn't work. Instead, I sketched nudes at the Art Students League a couple of times a week, and learned about anatomy. I joined my mother for lunch at her club, but I didn't belong to any clubs or organizations, and my friends were far-flung, except for Muffie. She lived a few blocks from me, and we got together often. We drank a lot. I often walked home with little memory of our conversation.

When I became pregnant with the first of Ned's and my two children, I was not aware of any restrictions on my drinking, so I drank heavily. As I was in the beginning stage of alcoholism, I would probably have drunk that way in any circumstance.

Pretty soon I started drinking alcohol in the middle of the day as well as at night. After all, I told myself, Ned and I drank cocktails before lunch and dinner, and when the sun fell over the yardarm at his parents' house or mine. In fact, I congratulated myself that drinking was an excellent solution to the problem of loneliness. It never occurred to me to talk to my parents or Ned about my emotions and actions. Wasn't I the luckiest girl in the world? Most of my high school and college friends were married and having babies, and they were happy too, the way they were supposed to be, weren't they?

Finally I got a volunteer job pushing a book cart to patients in a big city hospital. Then I landed a part time paid job at a non-profit foundation that helped foreign students study and live in the United States. The foundation was throwing a huge charity ball, and my work consisted of typing names and addresses of potential guests all day long. I had learned typing at school, and could speed along at 45 words a minute. (I thought this was fast.) The job was boring, so I drank at lunch with other employees, and learned the lesson that if I drank even one drink at lunch, I would inevitably get drunk later at home. If I didn't drink at lunch, I might not drink later. I didn't know I was learning by experience about the parameters of the disease of alcoholism first-hand; I had a constitution that was susceptible to the phenomenon of craving set off by the dangerous first drink.

My mother was learning the same lessons in New Jersey, but neither of us was close to admitting to each other or anyone else that anything was wrong. Dad was increasingly ill, and Ned and I drove out to the Hill often to see him. Dad looked as if he had been put through a wringer, drawn and pale, a shadow of his former athletic self. He sat on the stairs and hoisted his way up tread by tread to the second floor and his bedroom. Increasingly, he couldn't do the things he loved: trout fishing, gardening, seeing his friends and family. When he died of kidney failure and a heart attack in 1963, it became apparent that he had been the glue of the family, holding it together, and without him the glue began to unstick. All of us drank more.

My mother stayed in the house in New Jersey for a year after my father died. There were books on the stairs and in piles on the floor of the living room, bedrooms, bathroom. She wrote about the agony she felt living in the empty house. She was attempting to write a children's book about Tad Lincoln. Tad was the engaging little boy with a cleft palate who rode through the White House in a cart pulled by his pet goat. She wrote my brother Phil in California, "I'm determined to write my book, no matter what. Every day I am so excited by what I have found in my research and by the thoughts I am thinking that by noon I am exhausted with the excitement and roam the empty house restlessly, making cups of tea for myself, climbing back up the stairs and wondering helplessly if perhaps I should have someone to help me compile the notes stuck in all the thousands of musty volumes, each one containing references to dozens of points in my story. All the subjects are mixed up in an endless mess of double and triple ranks of bookcases. I haven't been able to see what is in the wall bookcases for a couple of years."

Finally she left the little Victorian house on the Hill and moved into her parents' now-empty brownstone on 78th Street in Manhattan. Gampy had died in his bed there; afterwards Granny kept asking as he lay there, "Isn't he sweet? Isn't he darling?"

My mother wrote her last two children's books at about the same time she moved to the city. She worked with the great children's book editor, Ursula Nordstrom, at Harper & Brothers. They became good friends and met often for lunch. The two books required my mother's loony kind of research and unusual characters. *Doctor Dick* featured a physician who had perpetual hiccups and who made house calls to give his patients peculiar and home-grown solutions to their problems, while they gave him suggestions for curing his hiccups. In *Billy the Barber*, she went to a barber's school and watched the student barbers shave balloons without popping them. To research a prospective book about garbage, she rode with the garbage man in the cab of his truck.

That was the end of my mother's children's book work. She was now completely obsessed with Lincoln and everything about him.

She wrote stories about Lincoln for *Colliers, Life,* and *The Saturday Evening Post*. Her writing for adults was similar to her children's work in that it was vivid and she often had a hook to draw the reader in. In "The Lost Doll of Appomattox," she wrote about a rag doll that was a silent witness to the surrender of the South at Appomattox. In "Lincoln's Lost Dog," she wrote about the "frisky mongrel named Fido who met a tragic end." (He was stabbed to death by a drunk.) In her ironic "Lincoln's Failure," she wrote about the Gettysburg Address, which was over in two minutes and only heard by a few people.

She visited Springfield, Illinois, Lincoln's hometown. A hands-on researcher, she climbed into a workman's trench and dug up mud at the level she guessed was the right level for Lincoln's era. She just had to know if the mud was sticky, or red, or some other adjective she could use in her writing.

My brother Phil had also become a fanatic. Together, they wrote a coffee-table book called *Twenty Days*, which was how long it took for Lincoln's body to be transported from Washington to his hometown. The book, published in 1965, had a foreword by the distinguished Lincoln scholar Bruce Catton. Scribners Bookstore on Fifth Avenue filled its windows with copies, and crowds of people came to look. Phil also wrote a book about my father, which was well received when it appeared in 1970. In a 1975 TV movie based on the book, Cliff Robertson played Phil, Jr., and Robert Preston of "The Music Man" fame played my father, who was depicted as often strumming a banjo, which he never did in his life.

My mother was invited to the White House for lunch as one of 100 Civil War historians. She was the only woman invited, and she was seated next to Gregory Peck. She also shook hands with President Lyndon B. Johnson, with whom she disagreed politically.

Soon after, *Life* magazine, where my brother Phil, Jr. was now Managing Editor, chose my mother to be the expert who would obtain copies of 19th century photographs from all over Europe for a year-end double issue chronicling the history of photography from its inception. The job was tremendously exciting, and my mother was at last able to call on her vast store of knowledge on the subject. First she was sent to Scotland, where the talented female photographer, Julia Margaret Cameron, had lived and worked. She moved on to England where William Henry Fox Talbot invented the first crude paper negative and where Edward

Muybridge took the first stop-motion photographs showing definitively that horses' four feet left the ground when galloping. Next she visited France where Niepce took the earliest photograph of all in 1826, and where Daguerre invented the photographic plate—called the daguerreotype, a treated copper plate that could hold an image.

I joined her at her expense for Italy, Austria, Germany, Denmark, and Holland. In Rome, we stayed near the Spanish Steps. She had treated herself to some new clothes and Louis Vuitton luggage and looked very smart. The amount of photographs we looked at was overwhelming, and soon she trusted me to make my own choices, which was immensely gratifying. As the trip evolved and with the help of *Life*'s foreign representatives, we searched for information in libraries, private collections, government agencies, institutes, and archives. We studied daguerreotypes, ambrotypes, ferrotypes, glass negatives, both original photographs and reproductions, transparencies, prints, documents, etchings, new and old newspapers, plans, drawings, and memorabilia. We talked with curators, heads of museums, photographers, historians, professors, librarians, and editors.

We also went clubbing with young *Life* correspondents, and I even danced the "frug," which was popular then. They arranged for us to visit the set of the 1967 movie "Taming of the Shrew" with Elizabeth Taylor and Richard Burton, where we watched them acting a scene. We went to the Vatican's vast Giglioli Collection and saw images from the 1860s. Giglioli traveled around the world photographing everything from nudes to family portraits, kings, potentates, maharajahs, sheiks, poverty, bound feet, samurai, American Indians, Africans.

This trip was my mother's swan song. She was drinking more, and I too was very sick from misuse of alcohol. My marriage was in trouble, but I wouldn't admit it. I showed up for teacher conferences at the children's schools, but I was full of shame and swollen from all the liquid calories I was pouring into my body.

My mother moved out of her parents' brownstone to a landmark building with a duplex living room. A beautiful apartment like this near her friends had been a dream, but she was not able to enjoy it. One night she broke her pelvis in a fall and was hospitalized. She had one of the first hip replacement surgeries. Afterwards, she was forced to give up her new apartment and move in with my sister in Massachusetts.

After my divorce, my own struggle with alcohol continued. I feared I would lose custody of my two children to my ex-husband, but after a terrible struggle, I entered recovery and stopped drinking. My first freelance job was obtaining photos for the children's book *ABC's of the Ocean* by Isaac Asimov. Later, I worked full time for a children's book publisher.

My mother died in 1979. I saw her a few days before she died at Nancy's. She was very ill with emphysema and had trouble breathing even though she was hooked up to an oxygen tank. The weather was chilly, and when I came into her room she held out her hands and took mine, warming them with her own. Her final words to me were "I...adore...you...." I had never doubted that.

At her burial in Staten Island, her granddaughter Dorothy zestfully read *Junket is Nice* out loud.

Six months later, I began writing children's books, not stopping until I had published over seventy of them with several different houses. Many of those books I illustrated as well. Among those that I am most proud of are the eight that I wrote and illustrated which were similar in format to *Pat the Bunny.*

In the early Eighties, my son and I visited the Hill. He was curious about where I had grown up, and I was eager to show him the landscape of my childhood. The people who now lived in the little Victorian let us walk through it. It seemed small and barely familiar. The tenants had a waterbed in one of the bedrooms. The Norton Memorial Eyebrow had been converted into a walk-in closet.

Outside, the cast-iron pipes in the water rams were cracked and the Pool was leaking. The underbrush in the woods was being decimated by voracious deer, which were overrunning the place. There was no trace of Dad's once-beautiful flowerbeds. My climbing tree where once I had hauled up books had been destroyed by the woolly adelgid, an insect that removes sap and injects a toxic spittle. A major highway, Route I-287, had been built parallel to the Hill. The roaring from its traffic never stopped, day or night. The beautiful tranquility of our Hill was gone.

A stone marker still showed where part of George Washington's Continental Army camped on the Hill during the winter of 1779-80, still the coldest winter on record in New Jersey, with seven blizzards in December alone and twenty-two altogether. It was the same winter when thousands in Washington's army died at Valley Forge. Hundreds perished there because smallpox developed, as well as dysentery. Twelve thousand soldiers, ill equipped for winter in ragged uniforms and insufficient footwear, lived in small huts on the Hill and at nearby Jockey Hollow. A thousand soldiers deserted. My brothers had searched for uniform buttons and cooking utensils in the faint depressions where the huts had stood, but they had never found any. Now there was no trace of the depressions.

In 2009, I planned another visit to the Hill. I wrote to Bill and Bertha's only surviving child, Pat, a world-class ornithologist and botanist. He was 97 and lived in Arizona. In his reply he asked about the gardens that he had designed as a boy. Could there still be signs of his work? "Was the little rounded foot bridge over the goldfish pond entering my rock garden destroyed? What about the perennial Christmas ferns I planted along the trail to the east? What about the 'Foxes' Table,' a large group of maidenhair ferns with almost a flat top growing so close together? Around the bottom of this I planted quite a few showy orchids. I am wondering in my old age if these things still exist."

In New Jersey I met with Jenny, Bill and Bertha's granddaughter and Pat's niece, who still lived in the area. She told me that in the Seventies, the Hill became a favorite place for drug addicts to make a connection. They gathered at the Apple Orchard, and sometimes stumbled into trees.

A search through knee-high weeds yielded the foot bridge, which had weathered into two fragile, rotten sticks laid across a dried-up hollow lined with rocks. The Christmas and maidenhair ferns were still growing. I couldn't approach the "Foxes' Table" as ticks were especially plentiful there.

Pat referred to our mutual love for the Hill and signed his letter, "in special bonds forever."

Nancy, Phil and Ken all died in the Eighties. It was a blow to lose my siblings, and I still miss them.

In that same era, parodies of *Pat the Bunny* started to appear, such as *Pat the Yuppies* and *Pat the Money*. The earliest ones were somewhat amusing, but then politics crept in, and bad taste. Pictures depicted Daddy's hairy stomach and worse: "Do YOU want to touch Bill Clinton's briefs?" "Paul prays for sex each night. Judy prays for erectile dysfunction." Judy pulls bloody intestines from a battered Bunny's stomach. "Now YOU gut the zombie," the text urges. Despite the sexual innuendo, bad taste, and vulgarity of many of them, they did sketch a picture of downward-spiraling cultural mores. I was relieved that my mother never saw any of the parodies.

In the Nineties, Muffie and I heard that the Big House on the Hill would soon be torn down. Bill and Bertha's family sold what was left of the estate to the Morristown Historic Park and the National Park Service. I visited again when the granite foundation stones, the characteristic brown shingles, and the jungle gym had been hauled away. It was disconcerting to find nothing familiar; only small trees sprouting on a level ground sprinkled with straw. Our little Victorian house was bought by someone who loved it, and who continues to improve it to this day. We had never owned it, but it was, without doubt, our home.

A special issue of *Newsweek* came out: "From Birth to Three: How to Build a Baby's Brain." *Pat the Bunny* was used as a major example of how reading aloud to children aids in their cognitive development.

In 2011, *Pat the Bunny* was made into an app for the new electronic media.

In the present, black bears creep down from the woods at night to rattle the Hill's few trash cans.

All these years, my longing for the Hill, as strong as the longing that took me away, was as much for the people as for the much-beloved landmarks. Now the people are gone, but those days on the Hill still seem enchanted, and the memories linger on.

One person stands out: I imagine her clearly, putting on her amber necklace and applying lipstick before going to a party, throwing a precious piece of work into the bath water, working on those stifling nights in her attic room, creating characters who are indelible.

Best of all, she invented a touchable rabbit that has captivated millions of American children in their earliest years.

Small Trees Sprouting